"This saga is a story about God. It is the account of God's unshakable faithfulness to those who suffer. It is the legend of how God hones and shapes each of His children into the image of His dearly beloved Son. It is a chronicle of grace."

JONI EARECKSON TADA, Joni and Friends

"As a documentary filmmaker, I have come across hundreds of interesting stories over the years. Very few have moved me like the epic and inspiring journey of Vanya Iliyn. I find it fascinating that, amidst the momentous events of World War II, God could be so taken up with the cause of a skinny orphan boy in China. But that is who He is."

GEORGE OTIS, JR., president, The Sentinel Group

"This book comes out of a great heritage, with exciting stories of faith that will build your faith and inspire your work for God."

LOREN CUNNINGHAM, founder, Youth With A Mission

"In giving voice to his father's firsthand account, Peter [Iliyn] reminds us of the suffering endured by many of God's people; inspires us to emulate the perseverance, courage, and faith of his father; and helps us to see the greatness of God in ways that make our own challenges seem small."

MIKE TREENER, international president, The Navigators

"I love spy stories—the danger, intrigue, and lots of adventure. Better yet, I love true stories with all the same elements. This book has them all! And underlying the intrigue and adventure in Russia and China is the story of God's grace. You will have a hard time putting this book down!"

FLOYD MCCLUNG, international director, All Nations

"After reading this story, I bowed my head and prayed, 'Lord, give me authentic, deep faith like Vanya's!'"

DR. BOB FETHERLIN, vice president for International
Ministries, The Christian and Missionary Alliance, U.S.

"What this world desperately needs is more dads like Vanya Iliyn, who, despite having to endure incredible hardships, became a very tender and loving father."

GEORGE DAVIDIUK, recording artist and
missionary evangelist to Ukraine

"One of the most impacting stories of the grace of God that I have read."

DR. LOUIE E. BUSTLE, director of Global
Mission, Church of the Nazarene

"*Out of the Far Corners* is a powerful testimony of God's faithfulness that will bring the reader into a deeper love and commitment to our heavenly Father."

DR. JERRY RANKIN, president emeritus,
International Mission Board, SBC

"An amazing story of perseverance and God's wonderful care and strength in all the circumstances of life."

L. JOHN BUENO, executive director,
Assemblies of God World Missions

"Peter Iliyn is a man of God and a strong leader. . . . *Out of the Far Corners* makes me even more impressed that God has His hand on Peter's life and ministry."

STEVE DOUGLASS, president, Campus Crusade for Christ

"This book will inspire young and old to be true to our ever-faithful God. To pray, believe, and persevere for the glory of God!"

PAUL FLEISCHMANN, president, National
Network of Youth Ministries

"This is an incredible story of God's faithfulness. Your heart will be warmed and encouraged as you read it."

BOB CRESON, president/CEO, Wycliffe Bible Translators USA

"This book is a grand slam! It is a riveting account of the faithfulness of God in the face of insurmountable odds."

CRAIG HILL, founder, Family Foundations International

"*Out of the Far Corners* is all you could wish for in a rip-roaring escape adventure. But Peter Iliyn has also given us a textbook for spiritual escape, as illustrated in young Vanya's release from the bitterness that could have followed years of abuse and being misunderstood."

JOHN SHERRILL, roving editor, *Guideposts* magazine

"Here is a saga that will touch you deeply. It will change the way that you look at life and strengthen your faith in God's character."

JIM STIER, director of the Americas, Youth With A Mission

"I loved reading the story of Vanya, a man who allowed so much hardship to make him better, not bitter. . . . This is a great read and I commend it to all."

DR. HANS FINZEL, president, WorldVenture

"An epic story of an orphaned boy's incredible journey to freedom. . . . God is standing in the shadows on every page."

DR. MICHAEL LOFTIS, president, Association
of Baptists for World Evangelism

"Peter Iliyn's story is in many ways my story. His dad and my dad were not only friends but fellow travelers down the same road. . . . These are lessons that we all need in overcoming and forgiveness. Hopefully another generation will have the opportunity of learning them as we did from our fathers."

AL AKIMOFF, YWAM Slavic Ministries

"This is a gripping and inspiring story. . . . It shows the heartbreaking sacrifice and agony of seeking freedom and illustrates the simple power of helping one another."

DR. RICK HICKS, North American area
leader, Operation Mobilization

"Vanya's life is a testimony that hearing the voice of God, endurance, perseverance, forgiveness, and faithfulness with a heart full of gratitude is the only path to true peace, happiness, and personal safety and security in this fallen world."

FRED MARKERT, international director, YWAM Strategic Frontiers

"Feeling a little overwhelmed? Sometimes we need a reminder of the greatness of God through an inspiring true story. . . . This is such a book, a page-turner that moves from darkness to dawn as the epic story of one man's life unfolds."

JOHN DAWSON, president, Youth With A Mission International

"A wonderful story of God's unfailing, miraculous manifestation of His faithful deliverance from seemingly impossible hardship and circumstances. You won't put the book down, and your heart will be drawn closer to the only true and living God."

DR. TED BARNETT, U.S. director of Africa Inland Mission

OUT OF THE FAR CORNERS

An Epic Tale of Rejection,
Grace, and Deliverance

PETER ILIYN

Foreword by Joni Eareckson Tada

YWAM PUBLISHING
Seattle, Washington

YWAM Publishing is the publishing ministry of Youth With A Mission. Youth With A Mission (YWAM) is an international missionary organization of Christians from many denominations dedicated to presenting Jesus Christ to this generation. To this end, YWAM has focused its efforts in three main areas: (1) training and equipping believers for their part in fulfilling the Great Commission (Matthew 28:19), (2) personal evangelism, and (3) mercy ministry (medical and relief work).

For a free catalog of books and materials, call (425) 771-1153 or (800) 922-2143. Visit us online at www.ywampublishing.com.

Out of the Far Corners: An Epic Tale of Rejection, Grace, and Deliverance
Copyright © 2011 by Peter Iliyn

Published by YWAM Publishing
a ministry of Youth With A Mission
P.O. Box 55787, Seattle, WA 98155

First printing 2011

Library of Congress Cataloging-in-Publication Data
Iliyn, Vanya.
    Out of the far corners : an epic tale of rejection, grace, and deliverance / [transcribed by] Peter Iliyn.
        p. cm.
    Life story of Vanya Iliyn, as told in his own words.
    ISBN 978-1-57658-545-0
    1. Iliyn, Vanya—Childhood and youth. 2. Russians—China—Biography. 3. Immigrants—China—Biography. 4. Children—China—Biography. 5. Orphans—China—Biography. 6. Abused children—China—Biography. 7. Xinjiang Sheng (China)—History—20th century. 8. Alma-Ata (Kazakhstan)—History—20th century. 9. Yining Xian (China)—History—20th century. I. Iliyn, Peter. II. Title.
    DS731.R9I55 2011
    362.96092—dc22   [B]2010046363

Printed in the United States of America.

To my papa. Your life stories changed my life.
And to my children: Lana Marie, Daniel Josiah, Paul Andrew, and
David James. Pass these stories on to your children's children . . .

ACKNOWLEDGMENTS

First of all, I wish to thank my wife, Luba, and our four incredible children—Lana, Daniel, Paul, and David—for their unwavering support of me as I labored to finish this book.

Many others also made this book possible, and to them I give my thanks: John Sherrill for spending five days with me instructing me how to write a book; Jannie Rogers for prodding me to write; Leland Paris for allowing my family to live on the Tyler YWAM campus as I began writing; Eunice Hansen and her late husband, Allan, founders of Christian Renewal Center in Silverton, Oregon, for allowing me to use their cabins as a place to write; Bill and Brooke Hicks for opening their home to me as a place to get away and write; my editors, Scott and Sandi Tompkins, for all the time and effort they put into making this book a reality; George Otis, Jr., for his creative suggestions regarding the content and title for my book; Peter Berg for his brilliant design work on my book cover; Luann Anderson and the entire YWAM Publishing editorial staff for a job well done in producing my book; and Barry Hon, Stu Sorenson, and Jim Musgrave for their timely financial support.

I also thank my father for the hundreds of hours he spent with us, his children, sharing his life story over and over and the countless hours he spent with me as I researched this book. And finally, thank you, Dad and Mom, for your many prayers, without which this book would never have become a reality. Thank you all.

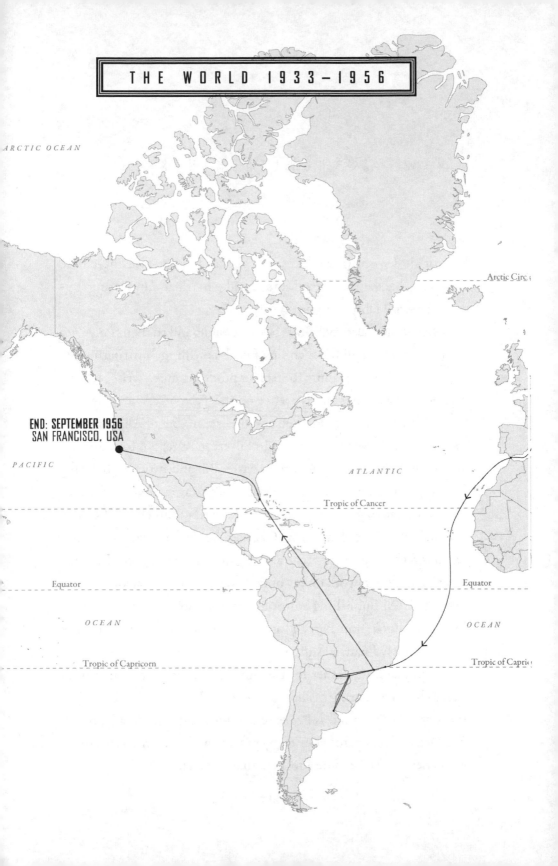

THE WORLD 1933–1956

ARCTIC OCEAN

Arctic Circe

END: SEPTEMBER 1956
SAN FRANCISCO, USA

PACIFIC

ATLANTIC

Tropic of Cancer

Equator

Equator

OCEAN

OCEAN

Tropic of Capricorn

Tropic of Capric

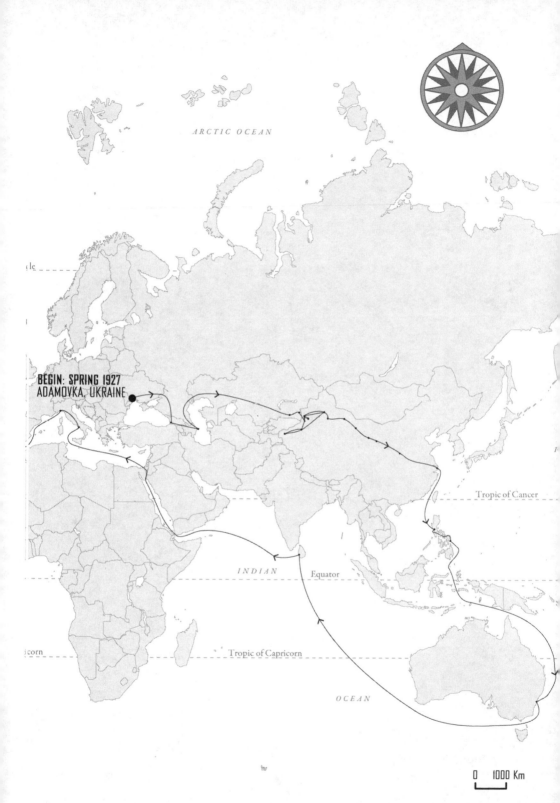

ARCTIC OCEAN

BEGIN: SPRING 1927
ADAMOVKA, UKRAINE

Tropic of Cancer

INDIAN

Equator

Tropic of Capricorn

OCEAN

0   1000 Km

CONTENTS

FOREWORD BY JONI EARECKSON TADA *xv*

HISTORICAL OVERVIEW *xix*

AUTHOR'S NOTE *xx*

PROLOGUE: MAY 1933—SINKIANG PROVINCE,
NORTHWESTERN CHINA *1*

PART 1

EARLY SPRING 1933—EAST OF ALMATY,
KAZAKHSTAN *7*

PART 2

FALL 1933—SOUTH OF GULJA, CHINA *53*

PART 3

JANUARY 1942—GULJA *137*

AFTERWORD *205*

FOREWORD

Ask the new generation of young people today about the cataclysmic events of the twentieth century and you'll likely draw a blank expression. Lenin . . . Churchill . . . Stalin? In modern school textbooks, these are obscure names given a mere page or two of explanation. Ask high schoolers about the Cold War, and they might tell you it was a battle over where to draw the Arctic Circle. Try Googling the Iron Curtain and you could get a MySpace profile about a punk-rock band rather than information about the historical division between the West and the Soviet Empire.

Twentieth century history is all but lost on a generation more preoccupied with the CliffsNotes version. It's time to revive the real story and take an up close and personal look at the lives of the people who truly made history in the last century. We need to hear about the stories of stalwart saints who crossed continents and cultures, surviving the brutalities of poverty and persecution in their quest for liberty and freedom.

And of all the stories, none will grip your heart and invigorate your faith quite like Vanya Iliyn's. It is more than a heart-racing account of an orphan boy's escape from the ironfisted tyranny of Stalin, or his family's journey from Ukraine across forbidding and dangerous lands into the desert of west China, or the unexplainable and miraculous encounters which the Iliyns experienced along the way. It is much more than that.

This saga is a story about God. It is the account of God's unshakable faithfulness to those who suffer. It is the legend of how God hones and shapes each of His children into the image of His dearly beloved Son. It is a chronicle of grace. For only the Lord Almighty could enable Vanya to interpret the many bruisings he received as blessings; only Providence could enable him to view his disappointments as heaven-sent disciplines and his trials as tests of faith from the hand of an all-wise and gracious God.

I need to be reminded of that. Even though I have lived as a quadriplegic in a wheelchair for more than four decades, I still need to be reminded of the tender hand of God at work in my own hardships. I need to be gripped by Vanya's story of courage and faith. I must learn it, rehearse it, and model it. And so must you, friend. Too many of us have become complacent in a culture that idolizes comfort. We've forgotten what it means to suffer for the sake of Christ—and to do it with grace, valor, and dignity. We need to learn how to smile not *in spite of* our problems but *because of* them.

The twentieth century is behind us and it's a different world now. Vanya would probably not recognize it. I take that back. He *would* recognize it. And he would know exactly what to do in the face of new wars that whisper of global holocausts: he would gently point people to the Savior, reminding them He is still the Way. He would remind us all of the old, old story that Jesus has conquered sin, no matter how ugly and pernicious it grows. And that soon—perhaps sooner than we think—He will close the curtain on hate and holocausts to welcome home His survivors.

Finally, though you hold in your hands a history book of sorts, please know that the following chapters are as current and compelling as ever. This is why I am pleased to commend to you *Out of the Far Corners.* It is for every person whose soul is threadbare and frazzled, for every individual who is staring into the jaws of their own affliction. And if you've gotten this far, it's for *you.* Go a little further and you will discover what I did.

If God's grace could sustain Vanya through horrible persecution, then His grace is sufficient for us. With His help you *can* survive. And Vanya would say you *will.* It is my prayer that through the following pages, you will begin to understand how the God of all history is writing *your* story through your own suffering. Just as He did for Vanya Iliyn.

"To this you were called, because Christ suffered for you, leaving you an example, that you should follow in his steps" (1 Peter 2:21).

Joni Eareckson Tada
Joni and Friends
Summer 2010

HISTORICAL OVERVIEW

In 1917 the Bolshevik Revolution swept across Russia, leaving major social upheaval in its wake. Vladimir Lenin, self-proclaimed leader of the revolution, ordered farms and industries to be collectivized. Vast numbers of people were displaced or imprisoned in this new communist world. Within a few years, Ukraine and other nations bordering Russia were swallowed up into the burgeoning Soviet Empire.

With Lenin's death in 1924 came the rise of an even more brutal tyrant, Joseph Stalin. Stalin's legendary purges against Jews, Christians, and numerous real and perceived enemies sent millions fleeing their homeland.

AUTHOR'S NOTE

This book tells the dramatic life story of my father, Vanya Iliyn, as told in his own words through my extensive research and interviews with my dad and those who knew him. It is a story of enduring faith amidst unbelievable life hardships.

Peter Iliyn

PROLOGUE

P APA, WHERE ARE YOU?"
I couldn't understand why my father wasn't with us. It seemed like only minutes ago he was carrying me through the flooded rice fields. As I peered out from behind a huge rock, all I could see were those dreaded open fields. So easy for the border patrols, both Russian and Chinese, to spot anyone trying to escape. Our weary band of refugees had made it safely so far on our long walk to freedom. But my papa was out there somewhere.

"Papa, where are you?"

That single question ricocheted through my mind as I searched the eyes of Misha, my twelve-year-old brother. Misha was over seven years my senior and always seemed to have answers. Surely he would know why our papa wasn't in hiding with the rest of the family.

"Not so loud, Vanya. Someone might hear us," Misha whispered as he lifted me up and pointed in the direction of the rice fields.

"Over there," he said. "See that mound? That's Papa lying on it."

I squinted, trying desperately to focus in the predawn darkness. Minutes later, as morning light reflected off the flooded fields, I noticed the raised mound. Sure enough, that was Papa's coat lying there. But where was he?

Only when the sun peeked over the horizon did I notice the shock of jet-black hair sticking out from my papa's coat. *That must be Papa's head,* I thought. *But why isn't he moving? He looks like he's sleeping, so peaceful, so vulnerable.* I wanted to run out to my papa. I wanted to feel his arms around me. I wanted Papa.

"Vanya, get down off the rock. Someone might see you." I reluctantly obeyed Misha and plopped down beside my two sisters, Marusia my oldest sister, and Lena, two years older than I. Marusia was always calm, even in fearful circumstances. Misha told me that Marusia had been accidentally dropped when she was three years old and severely broke her left hand. Since no doctors were available, her broken bone had become infected and never healed properly. That's why her left hand looked so awkward, almost as though someone had twisted it grotesquely. Her hand was always festering, and yellow pus oozed out of a persistent sore. But she commanded respect, and at age thirteen she was given much of the responsibility of caring for us.

Lena had eyes that were as black as her hair, with dark circles around them. Those eyes made her appear serious, like she was always in deep thought about something. She was a spunky girl, never lacking for something to say. But now she sat with us in silence, four hungry children in ragged clothes, clinging together in fear and hope.

Other families huddled nearby. As I noticed one father gently comforting his children, my own heart longed for the comfort of my father and mother. Papa was lying all alone out in the rice field and Mama . . . where was Mama?

The events of the past few days were a blur in my four-and-a-half-year-old mind. I remembered that Mama had crossed the border with us into China. Our group, forty-six people in all, had very little food and water when we fled by night from Zharkent, a city in the Soviet Republic of Kazakhstan, some twenty kilometers from the Chinese border.

Night after night we had all walked to get to this strange and lonely place, how many days I couldn't remember. These were terrible days, days I wanted to forget. I know we got lost along the way and nearly died of thirst. It seemed like some of the younger children cried the whole way. I cried, too, but most times I tried not to let it show. Crying did no good, but sometimes I got so sad because of the heat, the hunger and thirst, and the fear and fatigue. Thankfully, we were now safely across the border and well hidden.

Yesterday at first light, four women, including Mama, had volunteered to walk to nearby villages to buy bread. The men stayed behind and guarded the children. When Mama left, I wanted to go, too, but my legs hurt so much I couldn't walk another step. The only thing I could do was wait and pray. Hour after anxious hour we scanned the horizon, hoping the women would return with food to satisfy our raging hunger. With each hour we grew more anxious and restless. Then Misha cried out. He was the first to spot the women on the horizon, and he and I dashed out to meet our mother. To our horror, she was not with them.

"Where's Mama?" we pleaded.

"Ah, she's probably still looking for bread," her friend Masha said. "I'm sure she will be back soon."

Papa's face fell when he heard that Mama had not made it back. In silence we ate the flat, round bread we were given, and our anxious papa urged us to pray.

Toward evening, Mama was still not back, and the leaders of our group wanted to move on. They were afraid we were too close to the border. We all knew the consequences of being arrested—the men would be sent back to face imprisonment, beatings, and possibly death. Our main church leader, Ivan Verhovod, said we needed to go much farther into China before we would be safe. Not knowing how far into China we needed to be, we could hear the clear sense of urgency in our leaders' voices as they instructed us to move out under cover of darkness.

I'll never forget the look in Papa's eyes as the group prepared to leave. He protested loudly, trying desperately to persuade the group to wait for Mama, but to no avail. I heard Ivan Verhovod say to him, "We need to leave now, and you need to trust God to bring Pelageya back."

Torn between waiting for Mama and going ahead with the group, Papa told us to prepare to leave. Marusia and Misha began packing our meager belongings and helping Lena and me get ready. I kept asking Misha when Mama was coming back, but his only reply was a pained, tearful glance. Marusia began to cry, but none looked sadder than Papa. I had never before seen him so heartbroken as the moment we resumed our journey. He was usually smiling and singing as we walked, but now he groaned and slumped noticeably.

It had been dark the night before when we stumbled out into that huge rice field. The leaders wanted to go around the field, but it was too wide. Because of the waist-deep mud, walking through it was painfully slow. Several times as Papa carried me through the field, he stumbled and dropped me. Someone finally noticed his struggle and scooped me up out of the mud and began carrying me.

"Hurry, everyone! The sun will rise soon!" I could see the worried look on the face of Ivan as he shouted these words. We were safe only as long as it was dark, and less than an hour of darkness remained.

"There!" someone shouted. "Let's hide in that ditch by the road."

Now I recalled how we had gotten to this muddy ditch. But why was Papa out in the middle of the rice field? My young mind just couldn't make sense of it. I asked Misha the same question, and he said, "When the leaders told us to run and hide in the ditch, Papa was too weak to go on. So they found a dry area in the field and laid him on it. That way no one would spot him."

As I slumped against the wall of the ditch, I noticed mud oozing from my shoes. Papa had twice repaired my shoes, always giving them back to me polished and looking like new. What would he think now of their awful condition? What would Mama think? Why hadn't she found us? Why wasn't Papa coming to join us? Why was this happening to our family?

Tears rolled down my dirty cheeks, and not even the comfort of my brother could stop them.

PART 1

EARLY SPRING 1933—EAST OF
ALMATY, KAZAKHSTAN

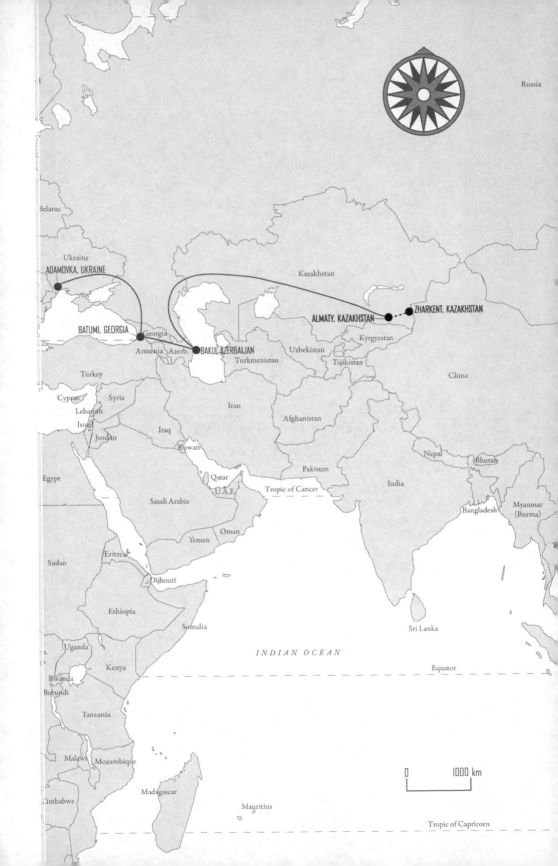

Russia

Belarus

Ukraine
ADAMOVKA, UKRAINE

Kazakhstan

ZHARKENT, KAZAKHSTAN

BATUMI, GEORGIA

Georgia

ALMATY, KAZAKHSTAN

Armenia Azerb.

BAKU, AZERBAIJAN

Uzbekistan

Kyrgyzstan

Turkmenistan

Tajikistan

Turkey

China

Cyprus Syria

Lebanon

Iran

Israel

Afghanistan

Jordan

Iraq

Kuwait

Nepal

Bhutan

Pakistan

Qatar

Tropic of Cancer

India

U.A.E.

Egypt

Saudi Arabia

Bangladesh

Myanmar
(Burma)

Oman

Yemen

Sudan

Eritrea

Djibouti

Ethiopia

Somalia

Sri Lanka

Uganda

INDIAN OCEAN

Rwanda

Kenya

Equator

Burundi

Tanzania

Malawi Mozambique

Mauritius

Madagascar

Zimbabwe

0   1000 km

Tropic of Capricorn

ONE

THROUGH THE FIRST years of my life there never was a time when my family felt truly safe. The older ones would whisper about the purges of some man named Stalin and tell of friends who had been taken away to God knows where. No one knew why they had been taken. They said the Bolsheviks didn't need a reason. Surely it wouldn't happen to us. Papa always said we Iliyns were good citizens, hard-working Christian people who wanted no trouble. But trouble and hunger and uncertainty seemed to dog our family everywhere we went. Even to the very borders of our homeland.

My earliest memory of my papa was of him coming home from work, always tired and hungry. He worked twelve-hour days as an electrician at the village power station. As soon as he would open the door, I would run barefoot across our mud-packed floor, yelling with glee. Up I would go into his arms, embracing him as tightly as I could.

"I caught a rabbit," Papa would say with a big grin, "and here's some bread for you and the others."

After gulping down the stale bread, I would look into Papa's dark brown eyes and ask, "Where did you catch the rabbit? Is this rabbit bread?" Marusia and Misha would always burst out laughing whenever I asked this question.

Laughter was more plentiful than food in our little village of Radivka, located near the Ili River. I wasn't old enough to remember how we got here, but Misha did tell me a little about the four-year trek our family made to get here from a tiny little village called Adamovka in Ukraine. He also told me I was born in Batumi, the Republic of Georgia, and that we got here with God's help, something I had often heard Papa and Mama say.

Our two-bedroom house was made of mud and straw. It belonged to the Sovxoz, a large communal cotton farm owned and operated by the government. We received food from the communal kitchen, but it rarely satisfied our gnawing hunger. Mama tried growing vegetables to supplement our meager diet.

Vasya, my younger brother, was born at this Sovxoz. He was three years younger than I and a sickly baby. Mama had tried giving him extra milk, but he never seemed to gain much weight.

Five other Christian families were living next to us. Our six families formed a little church, and we would gather each Sunday, sing songs, and listen to preaching, often delivered by Papa or one of the other men.

On holidays like Christmas and Easter we would travel on wagons to Zharkent, Kazakhstan, where we would attend the large church for special services. I always looked forward to these trips. I especially enjoyed seeing Uncle Mitrofan (Papa's brother) and Aunt

Maria. Mitrofan always treated us well, and on these holidays Aunt Maria would usually give us cookies or pieces of sugar. Up until then I had never before seen sugar.

Mitrofan and Maria had been the first in our family to flee from Ukraine, and we followed them to Kazakhstan. My *dedushka* (Papa's father) had also come to live with them. Even during these festive times, Dedushka seemed to be lost in his own thoughts. Misha said it was because his wife had been killed right before he left Ukraine.

Another thing I recall from those times was Papa and Mama speaking to us about China, a country not far from our village. They said it was the place God was leading us to. They said He would give us white bread, sugar, honey, and milk in China. Soon I found myself dreaming of China, of mountains of sugar and fields of soft, white bread.

One evening as we children knelt beside our bed for evening prayers, Papa told us God had spoken to him that it was time to go to China.

"YES!" I squealed.

"Shush, Vanya!" Papa said. "We must keep our plans secret. If the police find out we're leaving for China, they will put me—maybe all of us—in jail." I surely didn't want Papa to go to jail, so I didn't tell a soul.

The next evening Mama gave us each an extra piece of black bread to eat. Then Papa gathered us beside our bed and knelt to pray. When he finished, he turned to us and said, "Tonight we're going to China." Misha and I and our sisters were beside ourselves with joy. I could almost taste the white bread and sugar of China.

That night we slipped away from our house around eleven o'clock. Papa and Mama didn't take much at all, only a change of clothes and some food. We simply walked out of our house, locked the doors, and left.

Our family of seven was joined by our neighbors, a woman named Mary Harinova, and her mother Sonia. Papa said if we kept moving we should reach the border by morning. As we walked through the night, we tried to keep hidden, and thankfully we saw no one. The grass and bushes near the border made it easy to hide. They were so tall I couldn't see over them when Papa let me walk beside him.

Soon after dawn we reached the Khorgos River, marking the border with China. Papa and Mama found a safe place for us children to rest. But the food was gone, and our growling stomachs found no rest. Papa pointed out some shepherds' yurts across the river, and Mama nodded. Minutes later Mama and Sonia, another neighbor who had joined our group, dashed across the river. Papa said they went to buy bread, and sure enough, when they returned about an hour later, Mama carried a stack of warm, round pieces of flat bread. My dream of abundant bread from China was coming true. Misha and I were so ecstatic that when Mama gave each of us a piece, we started stuffing our hungry mouths. Papa stopped us with a cold stare and motioned for us to bow our heads. Such a long prayer it was for children holding warm, soft bread in their hands.

At his "amen" we started to eat, but now Mama stopped us. "When we were praying, God spoke to me and said we shouldn't stop here. We must cross the border and then eat."

I certainly hadn't heard God say anything, but Mama seemed convinced. Our neighbor Mary protested loudly and prevailed on Papa to let us stay and eat the bread while it was warm. I was quite happy to stay there and eat, but I wondered why Papa didn't say anything in Mama's defense.

As we began eating, Mary slipped away to draw water from a nearby pond. Before she came back, Vasya had started crying loudly. Mama tried desperately to quiet him, but he cried all the louder. Then we heard another sound, a fearful, thundering sound that sent chills through my body—horses galloping straight for us!

Vasya kept crying, and we had no place to hide. Suddenly two black horses swept up almost on top of us. I was so frightened by these huge beasts I dropped my piece of bread. Upon the horses were two uniformed Russian border guards, both grinning as they peered down at us.

"What have we here?" one guard with a thick black mustache bellowed. "Where do you think you're going? To China?" Both men began to roar with laughter.

Before I knew what happened, the guards dismounted and began going through all of our belongings. What little money Mama had brought for the trip they took.

Mary, who hadn't gotten back from the water pond, never did come back. I think she probably heard the commotion and ran across the border. Her mother called desperately for her but to no avail. The guards even looked for Mary, but never found her.

After taking everything away from us, including our bread, the guards herded us for about five kilometers till we came to their head-quarters. I'll never forget how they stripped all of us and took nearly everything we had. Before we arrived, I saw Sonia giving Mama two gold coins and asking her to please hide them for her. Mama swallowed one of the coins and hid another in her hair. The guards didn't find these coins. Mama also had a twenty-ruble note, which Misha hid inside his shoe.

The guards took Papa and placed him in a separate room with the other men. Mama and the rest of us were shoved into a small room already half full with other families caught trying to escape to China. One family wore strange little caps and veils. Mama said they were Muslims. Also, Jewish families and other Russians like us were all huddled together, looking scared and hungry.

During the three days they kept us locked in this room, all we had to eat was watery soup and tiny pieces of stale bread. Occasionally, the guards would let us go outside within a small fenced area, but there was no shade and the afternoon sun was unbearable. We were constantly hungry and thirsty. Once when Misha and I were standing near the fence, he noticed the guards feeding their pigs and dogs. One dog was given a bigger piece of bread than they gave our entire family. As the dog ran by us, Misha pulled the fence up and dashed off after it. The soldiers began yelling and running toward Misha, but before they could catch him, he had scared the dog enough to make it drop the bread. Picking the bread up, Misha quickly scrambled back under the fence and triumphantly presented it to Mama.

"You can't do that," one of the soldiers yelled.

"We're hungry," Misha said as he turned his back to the soldier. I saw him grin at me as he walked away from the fence.

During those three days, more families were brought to the police station until there was no room for anyone else. We hadn't seen Papa since they took him away. On the third day they rounded up all the women and children in a large field outside the station. There must have been sixty of us that hot, dusty morning.

Misha suddenly pointed and yelled, "Look, there's Papa!"

The soldiers were herding the men past us and onto the road toward Zharkent. As they shuffled by, Papa waved to us. He didn't look well at all, but he did manage a smile. The dust was so thick that Papa soon disappeared.

The soldiers kept us in this field for over two hours, giving us neither food nor water. Misha asked Mama to let him go and beg for bread in the surrounding villages. Mama was afraid we would leave before he came back, but Misha finally persuaded her to let him go. I wanted to go, too, but I knew Mama would never agree.

Misha had been gone less than an hour when the soldiers came and began yelling for us to start moving. Mama began frantically looking for Misha and crying out his name. But Misha never came. As the soldiers herded us forward, Mama began to cry. I didn't understand what was happening, but as we walked, I heard Mama praying, "O God, please don't let me lose both my husband and my son. Bring them back."

"Mama, where are we going?" I asked.

"We're going back to Zharkent," Mama replied.

"Will Papa and Misha be in Zharkent?"

"I hope so, but I really don't know." Mama's eyes were all red, and I could see tear stains all over her collar. She kept squeezing her eyes with her fingers and constantly looking back. I think she was looking for Misha.

At times the soldiers would push us to walk faster, and Mama would pick me up and carry me. My sisters carried Vasya and what meager belongings we still had. As trucks passed by on the narrow dirt road, we'd be covered in dust, which stuck to our sweaty skin. Mama gave us what little water she had saved in a small tin can. The soldiers gave us nothing. They just kept pushing us forward.

As we neared a small village, a truck came up behind us honking its horn. The truck was piled high with sacks of cotton. Perched on top of them, waving his hands frantically and yelling, was Misha.

"I'm okay, Mama. I'll see you at the next town. Don't worry about me."

Misha's voice trailed off as the truck passed us in a cloud of dust. But Mama was now smiling. God had answered her prayer.

The soldiers started yelling at us again. Only this time they were telling us we were free to go. They just walked away and left us there in the middle of the road. Mama told us the soldiers had tired of trying to make the women and children walk faster and decided to leave us on our own. I don't think they cared whether we lived or died. But Mama did. She kept urging us to walk faster as evening was approaching.

Right before nightfall we entered another small village. Mama said we needed to find a place to sleep and hopefully some food and water. Then we noticed the figure of a boy standing in the doorway of an abandoned house. It was Misha! As we approached the house, he ran up to us and hugged each one of us.

Tears flooded down Mama's face, and Misha asked, "Why are you crying?"

"They've taken Papa off to prison in Zharkent," Mama said. "We don't have any food or a place to sleep. What will we do tonight?"

"Don't worry, Mama. I've found us a place to stay. Follow me."

Misha led us to an old, abandoned house on the outskirts of the village.

"There weren't any windows or doors on this house when I found it," Misha said, "but I made some doors out of old boards and curtains out of discarded material that I found along the roadside." Misha had even made some beds for us out of hay. The house was cold, but at least we had a place to spend the night.

It was getting dark fast. Mama told Misha to start a fire while she looked for food. She peered out the window and saw a small lighted farmhouse not too far away. "I'm going over to that farmhouse to barter for some flour."

I watched Mama reach into her dress pocket and carefully pull out a beautiful blue scarf. Mama had been protecting this scarf, which she had received years earlier as a gift from her mother. As she stroked it gently, Marusia and I realized Mama was going to trade her most precious possession to get food for us. How could she make such a sacrifice? And what a sacrifice it was, for she returned with just three cupfuls of wheat husks. By then Misha had a fire going, and Marusia had picked a few green apples from a tree outside. Mama peeled the apples and mixed them in with the husks, hoping the apples would help the blintzes stick together. They didn't. Mama cried as she cooked our simple meal. I don't know whether it was because of the scarf or because she was missing Papa or because of our uncertain future. We were so hungry that we didn't mind the tart taste, and we gladly ate every blintz Mama fried up.

That evening as we lay on our hay beds, each of us had a terrible stomachache. I cried for hours as my stomach was seized with pain. Marusia and Lena tossed and turned all night. Only toward morning did our pain subside.

In the morning we continued our trek to Zharkent. After walking for most of the day, we arrived back at our Sovxoz. As we approached our house, we noticed people inside. Misha ran up to the door and went inside. To our amazement, our neighbors were sitting around a fire they had built on the dirt floor—right in the middle of our house. They were boiling a rabbit inside a big pot and were as surprised to see us as we were to see them.

"We thought you had left for China," they said, "and your house was abandoned. Please forgive us for this intrusion."

Mama said it was all right and gladly accepted some of their boiled rabbit and soup as a gift from them. After eating the rabbit, we all quickly fell asleep.

The next morning we continued on to Zharkent. Since we had no money or food, we stayed in the homes of Christian friends. I remember staying with the Shevchenkos, because they were especially kind to us. Alex Shevchenko was sixteen years old, and often after work he would play with Misha and me. Mama would daily bring food to Papa in jail. She told us Papa looked very tired and encouraged us to pray for him. Papa sat in jail for three weeks before they released him. Once outside, the only work Papa could find was in the rice fields. He was paid mostly with rice, and all we had to eat was the rice porridge Mama made for us.

While living in Zharkent, we attended church with six or seven other families, a total of forty-six adults and children. Church services were held every Sunday morning and evening and every Wednesday evening. We gathered in a rented house on a street lined with beautiful birch trees. The church was located next to a large, open-air market, which seemed like it never closed. The market was always full of people buying and selling vegetables, fruit, all sorts of animals, and other things. Many of the people wore little caps on their heads and had dark skin, not at all like us fair-skinned Russians. They seemed more like the people we had met while being held in the border jail. Papa called them *Musulmani* (Muslims).

I recall that as we went to church, we would often walk by the police station. Each time, Misha would speak to me in hushed tones about how the police were spying on the Christians and were looking for any chance to arrest people planning to escape to China.

I didn't know it, but Papa and the other men of the church were already asking God about a new plan of escape to China. When Papa told us after prayers one night, I was shocked. If he was caught trying to escape a second time, the punishment would be even more severe. He was still so weak from his time in jail that I couldn't imagine him walking so far. Escaping to the border would be a much farther walk than returning to our place at the Sovxoz.

Each night Papa would pray for strength, saying, "Dear God, I'm weak and tired, but I don't want to be left behind. Please speak to us also and lead us out with the group."

I remember Papa and Mama often praying with the Shevchenkos and Dumanovskys till late into the night, asking God for clear direction on when and how to leave for China. After one such prayer meeting, Papa gathered us together and said, "Tomorrow God will lead us into China."

I couldn't sleep that night as I once again began dreaming about sugar and white bread. I remembered the piece of soft bread I almost got to eat before it was taken away by the border guards. *This time,* I thought, *I'm going to eat that bread as soon as I get it in my hands.*

Papa went to work in the rice field the next morning just as if it were another day. "We don't want to arouse any suspicion," he told Mama as he left.

When he returned home that afternoon, our family sprang into action like rabbits on the run. It wasn't hard for Mama to get us ready, because we didn't own much. All she took for our trip were clothes, some jugs of water, and three loaves of black bread.

"The plan is for us to meet the others in our church building and leave for China from there," Papa told us.

As we walked by the police station, I looked straight ahead, praying we wouldn't be noticed. I hoped to never again see the inside of a police station.

As evening neared, other people began arriving at the church until all forty-six of us were together. Most of us children were excited, but the leaders appeared very serious. I noticed the mothers trying desperately to keep their small babies from crying. My little brother,

Vasya, cried too. He still looked so small and sickly. Mama held him constantly, feeding him rice porridge and trying to keep him quiet.

I noticed we didn't sing songs like we usually did during church services. Misha said it was because of a fear of being discovered by the police. Even our prayer times were quieter than normal.

Then one of the leaders spoke up, saying he had received this word from God: "Listen, My little children, stand strong in your faith, for tonight I will lead you out. You will go with singing and great rejoicing."

I remember hearing several people say, "How could this be? There are people all around us, and police are patrolling the streets. They'll hear us and capture us. We'll all be sent to jail. This can't be God."

But others, including Papa and Mama, seemed to believe this was God speaking, and they continued praying. Then came another prophecy I'll never forget. In a strong voice one of our leaders said, "Hear the Word of the Lord: 'Children, I will lead you out at 1:00 AM.'"

We waited, and at midnight a violent storm suddenly struck Zharkent. The wind blew so hard that I thought the birch trees outside would surely break. The shrieking wind drowned out the sounds of people running home from the marketplace, leaving the streets ghostly and empty.

Then came God's final instruction: "Children, leave now, for My hand will protect you."

Ivan Verhovod opened the door, and we all started slowly exiting the building. Papa carried me as we stepped outside into a howling storm. Leaves blew everywhere, and it was beginning to rain. I could hear the rumbling of thunder in the distance. By the time everyone had left the building, we had formed a single-file line two blocks long, marching right through the middle of town. Several young girls near the front began praising God loudly, but the wind was so strong we could barely hear them.

And so God led us out of Zharkent without the police or anybody else noticing. As we came to the outskirts of town, the city bell tower tolled 1:00 AM. God had kept His promise.

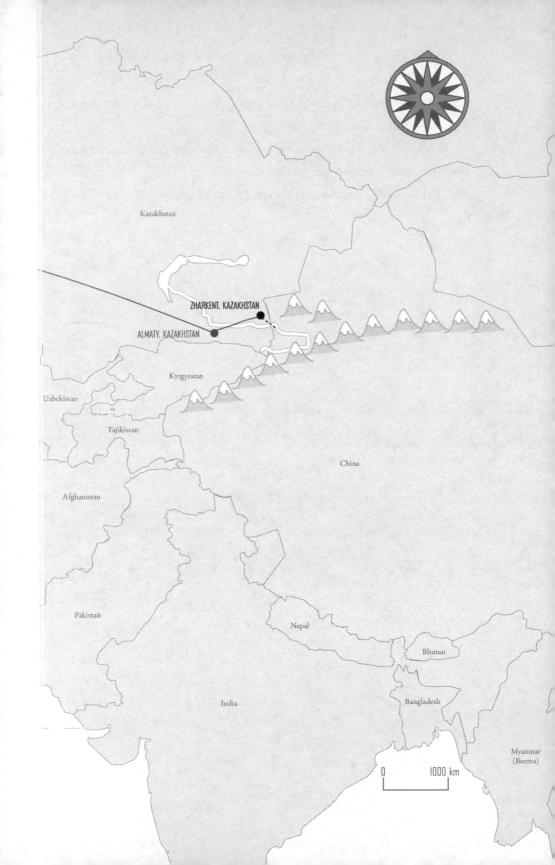

ZHARKENT, KAZAKHSTAN

ALMATY, KAZAKHSTAN

Kazakhstan

Kyrgyzstan

Uzbekistan

Tajikistan

China

Afghanistan

Pakistan

Nepal

Bhutan

Bangladesh

India

Myanmar
(Burma)

0   1000 km

OUR LEADER, IVAN VERHOVOD, was a grandfatherly sort of man with a warm and friendly face. Both Papa and Mama spoke well of him and consented willingly when he led the group by a more roundabout desert route to avoid detection. Even though no one from our group had ever traveled this route to China, we all sensed God's sovereign hand leading us. Traveling at night and sleeping during the day became our routine. Our route took us through sand dunes and little shrubs. Every time we approached a fork in the road, the leaders would pray and God would direct us which way to go. As long as we obeyed Him, we progressed closer toward the Chinese border. But some in our group began to complain and insisted they knew best which way we should go.

One of these times, Ivan yielded to these complainers, and we found ourselves wandering for days in the wrong direction. During this horrible journey, we were without water for three days and nights. My throat was so dry I could barely speak. Misha, Marusia, Lena, and I all had cracked and bleeding lips. But little Vasya was suffering the most. He was becoming weaker by the hour.

We all begged Mama for water, but she just stared at us with sad, empty eyes. There was no water. What could she do? When Vasya began whimpering, I saw Mama kneel down and bring a moist rag up to Vasya's mouth.

"What's Mama doing?" I asked Papa.

"She's trying to keep Vasya alive."

"So why is he sucking that rag?"

Papa's eyes welled up with tears. "The only water Mama has is her own urine." As he said this, he began to weep uncontrollably.

Vasya died a short while after this. Mama wrapped him in a blanket, and Papa buried him in a shallow grave that he dug with his own hands. We all cried and prayed next to his little grave.

On the third day, no one in our group could go any farther. Not only had the hot desert air sucked every bit of moisture out of us, but also we had run out of bread. Some of the older people began slumping to the ground, unable to take another step. Children cried loudly, begging their mothers for water, for bread. We were in a strange desert in the middle of the night with no water source anywhere nearby.

Without anyone telling us what to do, we all began falling to our knees and crying out to God. Mama pleaded with God to give us water. She began yanking at her hair, like she was pulling it out. As Papa fell to his knees, he placed me on the sandy ground. My eyes were fixed on Mama, but I, too, knelt down and began to cry, "O God, please give us water or we will all die!"

With nothing but sand dunes all around us there was no natural way out of this predicament. Only God could save us. And in the midst of our wailing, He spoke again: "Children, get up off your knees. Walk fifty meters, turn left, and walk one hundred meters and begin to dig."

The men near the front of the group scrambled to their feet and began running through the sand to the exact spot indicated by God. All of us gathered around as they dug with their bare hands. Everyone was hopeful, especially since bulrush was growing near this spot. The hole was several feet deep when the sand became wet. Handfuls of this sand were scooped up and placed into rags and scarves and given to desperate mothers who tried squeezing out precious drops of water into the mouths of their crying children.

Papa joined in the digging. As the men dug deeper, suddenly a cry went out throughout the group: "Water, there's water in this hole!"

Even before the water cleared up, people began lapping it up, filling their pots, pans, and teapots with sandy water. We drank the water, poured it on our heads, and began laughing. Our cries of desperation turned into sounds of joyous singing. Once again, God had answered our prayers.

We spent three days around that water hole, resting and replenishing our thirst. During our evening prayer times, I heard Papa say, "Let's be thankful to God for answering our prayers, but let's not repeat this mistake again. Disobeying God is always wrong."

The day we left that water hole, some of the men wrote on a piece of wood and tacked it onto a stick next to our water hole.

"What's that sign say?" I asked Misha.

Misha studied the sign and read, "To all who pass by and are in need of water, drink this fresh water provided for us by God. May 1933."

As we left that water hole, I looked back, wondering whether I would ever again be as thirsty. It didn't seem so. The closer we got to the border, the more green and watered the land appeared. We arrived at the Chinese border about midnight, and as we reached the

Sailimu River, several of the people in the front hurried across. Then the forward movement stopped. Papa, still holding me, ran up from the back, trying to find out what happened. Our leader was pointing his finger, saying, "Look! Rice fields ahead. If we go straight, we must walk through water and mud. To the right, exactly the same. To the left is a Chinese border patrol bunker. What should we do?"

Ivan Verhovod's wife, Masha, took him by his shoulders and said, "Follow me!" She led us straight across the border and turned left—right toward the patrol bunker. As we walked by the bunker, we heard a dog barking but did not see any Chinese soldiers. After a short while, we exited the rice fields. An audible sigh of relief was let out by the entire group. We were finally in China!

Even though everyone was excited about arriving, our gnawing stomachs reminded us that we could die of hunger here if we didn't find food. After we had rested behind some sand dunes till morning, several of the men noticed some yurts off in the distance.

"There's probably food there," they said. All I could think about was biting into a piece of that white round bread I had never gotten to taste.

Mama and three other women agreed to search for food. Mama knelt down and gave each of us a kiss on our forehead, and then she was gone. Mama said she would bring us white bread. Oh, how I wanted that white bread!

"VANYA, PUT YOUR shoe back on. Look, they've gone to get Papa."

Misha's words had shaken me out of my wandering thoughts, and I frantically worked to get my shoe back on. I kept bumping into Lena as I tried balancing on one foot. Misha and Marusia were peering up over the lip of the ditch in the direction of the rice fields.

"Let me see!" I yelled.

As my foot finally squeezed into my shoe, I bounded up next to Misha. He lifted me up just high enough for my nose to rest on the edge of the ditch. I could smell the damp ground and feel the wet grass up against my nose.

"What are they doing to Papa?" I asked Misha.

"Looks like they're wrapping him in a blanket," he said.

"Maybe he's wet and cold?" Marusia said.

We held our breath as the two men carrying Papa waded through waist-deep water and mud on their way toward us. As they got closer, I noticed Papa's right arm plop down into the water and dangle there as the men labored to carry him out onto dry land. As they laid Papa on the ground, I strained my neck to see his face.

"Misha," I said, "Papa's face is covered with the blanket. Why?"

Misha didn't reply. He just stared at Papa lying on the ground. I noticed tears forming in the corner of his right eye and suddenly, like the overflowing of a dam, Misha's tears rolled uncontrollably down his cheeks.

"What's the matter, Misha?"

"Papa is . . . is dead," he whispered.

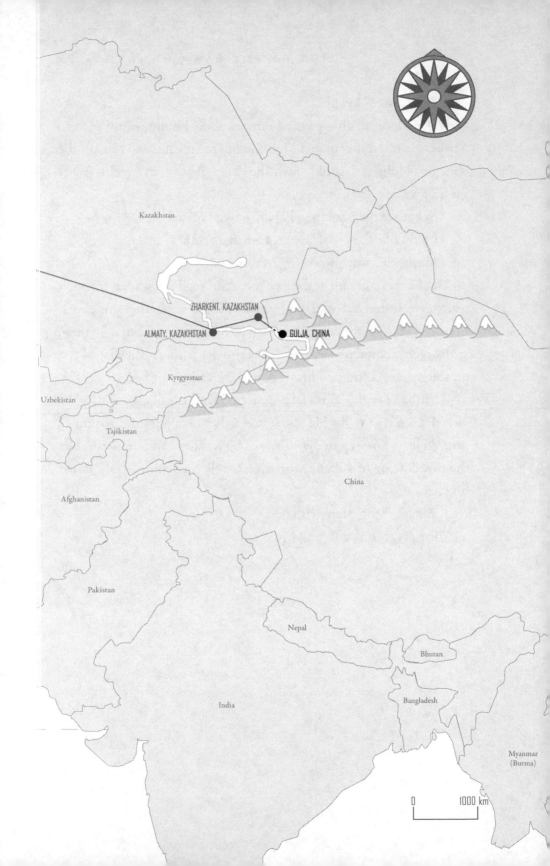

ZHARKENT, KAZAKHSTAN

ALMATY, KAZAKHSTAN

GULJA, CHINA

Kazakhstan

Kyrgyzstan

Uzbekistan

Tajikistan

Afghanistan

China

Pakistan

Nepal

Bhutan

India

Bangladesh

Myanmar
(Burma)

0   1000 km

THREE

P APA IS DEAD."

Marusia and Lena, after hearing Misha's words, both began to cry. But somehow the words didn't make sense to me. I didn't know what to do. Several of the men began digging a hole with their hands under a large bush. I then remembered the hole Papa had dug out in the desert, the hole Vasya—wrapped in a blanket—had been placed in. And now Vasya was gone.

A blanket. Papa is wrapped in a blanket. It suddenly hit me.

"No!" I yelled. "Don't put my papa into that hole."

My screams startled the men. I tried to claw my way out of the ditch to stop them, but Misha kept pulling me down. "Vanya, stop it," he said. "Papa is dead, and there's nothing you can do about it."

As I slid back down into the ditch, I began to sob. Marusia picked me up and held me tightly. I could feel her tears rolling down my neck and her heaving chest as she, too, cried deeply. Through my tears I could see Lena sitting on the ground, hugging her knees close to her chest and sobbing.

I knew it was Misha speaking but could barely recognize his crackling voice. "Remember what Papa and Mama always told us," he said, wiping his eyes on his sleeve. "Death is only a temporary separation. We will soon meet again in heaven."

I knew I would see Papa in heaven, but I wanted to run to him now, to feel his arms around me *now*. Marusia pulled me into her arms, but I kept crying louder with each breath.

"Quiet down, guys, someone's coming!"

In response to Misha's command I quickly wiped my eyes and nose on my jacket sleeve and stood up.

"Let me see, let me see."

Misha once again lifted me just high enough to see over the edge of the ditch. Off in the distance I saw a man walking through the field with some type of curved tool in his hands. He was walking straight at the three men that were digging a hole for Papa. They must have also seen the man, because they stopped digging and stood to face the approaching stranger.

"Let's crawl up next to the bush and see what this is all about," Misha said.

I didn't wait for a second invitation. We scrambled out of the ditch and crawled up next to the bush just as the stranger was approaching. The man wore a square, wine-colored cap on his head and sported a black, bushy mustache under a large, lumpy nose. His dark skin and big hands were as well-worn as elephant hide. In his right hand he firmly held a battered yet recently sharpened scythe. He didn't look mean, though, and smiled as he greeted the men in broken Russian.

"Salaam alaikum!" he then said.

"Peace to you too," they replied to the Muslim greeting.

"My name is Sayjan. I'm the owner of this field, and I noticed you digging in it. What are you doing, and what's in that blanket?"

Alex Shevchenko and Lueva Dumanovsky began answering at the same time. After a quick glance at each other, Alex spoke. "Do forgive us for digging a hole in your field. We were only trying to bury one of our friends who died this morning."

"How did he die?"

"We really don't know," Alex said. "He seemed so weak these past two days and was constantly grasping his right side. It may be that his appendix was hurting him. He also lost his wife yesterday and was struggling to keep watch over his four children."

"Where's your home, and who are you?" Sayjan asked.

"We are Russian refugees and just this morning crossed the border," Lueva said.

Sayjan looked thoughtfully at our men and said, "You look like you could use some food. Come with me and bring the body of your friend. You don't want to bury him under this bush anyway, because there are wild dogs around here. I'll show you a burial ground, and there you can put your friend to a final rest."

"We are grateful to you for your offer of help," Alex answered, bowing slightly. "I want to warn you that there are forty-six adults and children in our group."

"That's quite alright," Sayjan answered. "My people are accustomed to large parties. Where is the rest of your group?"

Alex pointed to his right and said, "They're all in that ditch."

Suddenly, with a big, arching swing of his scythe, Sayjan exclaimed, "Come, my friends. Let us go to my home."

Misha grabbed my arm and half dragged, half carried me back to the ditch. I noticed that Papa's body was left behind as Alex and Lueva led Sayjan toward the ditch. Alex introduced him to the whole group. With a big grin Sayjan said, "You are all welcome to my home. Come."

Everyone grabbed their bags and began moving out of the ditch. The fear and frustrations of the past few days gave way to a new atmosphere of anticipation and excitement. As we marched toward Sayjan's house, Alex and his parents kept us Iliyn children close to their family.

I had seen yurts like Sayjan's from a distance but never this close. This yurt looked more like a large tent than a house. Its wooden frame was wrapped in a thick, coarse felt. Sayjan directed us to sit on fresh hay scattered on the ground. I couldn't help noticing a young girl sitting next to a horse, which she appeared to be milking.

"Misha, what's that girl doing?" I asked.

"She's milking the mare," Misha replied. "The milk she gets is then left to stand for several days till it ferments, and then they drink it. They call it *kumiss*."

"Yuk!" I said. "It must taste awful."

Soon Sayjan's workers brought us fresh-baked round bread, milk, and a variety of vegetables. As I ate my share, I kept thinking about that first piece of round bread I never got to eat. I savored each bite, closing my eyes as I swallowed. It tasted even better than I had imagined it would.

After breakfast, Sayjan led us to a burial ground not too far from his home. There, with the help of Sayjan's workers, a grave was dug. Ivan Verhovod read several scriptures and said a few kind words about Papa. He then led us in song.

Papa was lying next to the open grave with his face exposed. Before he was buried, all of us filed by and looked at him one last time. Marusia held me as we filed by. Papa's eyes were closed, and he had a peaceful look on his face. I touched his face but immediately drew my hand back because his face was so cold. As Marusia led me away, I looked back and waved goodbye.

Sayjan's workers gave us enough bread to last all day. We even had enough for breakfast the following morning. As we prepared to leave, Sayjan came up to us.

"Are these the children who lost their father?" he asked Alex.

"Yes," Alex replied.

"How old are they?"

"Marusia is thirteen, Misha is twelve, Lena is seven, and Vanya is almost five."

"Misha is almost as dark as my people." Sayjan placed his hand on Misha's head as he spoke. "Why don't you leave him with me? I don't have any children of my own, and I'll care for him like a son."

"They still have a mother. She's not here right now, but she's coming," Alex said.

"If you leave him with me, I'll even help them as a family when they find their mother."

I began to feel sick to my stomach as I listened to them discussing a further breakup of my already shattered family.

"We can't make that decision," Alex said. "What will we say to their uncle and aunt who live in Gulja?"

"Well, then, leave Lena with me. She's also dark-skinned."

"You've been so kind to us, but we just can't do this—at least not until we consult with their family in Gulja," Alex said.

I was very glad that Misha and Lena weren't left behind.

Sayjan finally gave up and showed us the road to Gulja. He gave us more bread and bade us farewell.

As our group walked along the dirt road, I could see high mountains to the south of us. Ivan Verhovod called them the Tien Shan and said the snows from those peaks watered this great desert valley.

More mountains were to the north, and some said there was a large lake. That was confirmed when three old Russian wagons came up behind us. Ivan found out that the men in the wagons were Russian fishermen returning to Gulja with no catch. They offered to give us a ride, and our older people and children got to ride all the way to Gulja, some forty-five kilometers, in these wagons.

It was dark by the time we arrived, and my back and bottom were aching after being jostled along that horrible, rutted road. Like Zharkent, this dusty place seemed to be a gathering spot for traders and travelers. There were Russians and Kazakhs, like those I knew from home, and the men also pointed out native Uygur people, some Chinese, and even a few Jews.

Gulja was divided in two by the Pelechinka, a spring-fed stream that flowed from the north into the Ili River. Situated on the west side of the Pelechinka was the new city, where many wealthier Russian-speaking Tatars lived. Everything to the east of the Pelechinka was called the old city and was populated predominately by Chinese who lived in poorly built huts made from mud, sticks, and thatch.

The fishermen dropped us off at a *caravanserai*, and I had hopes of stretching out on a bed to sleep. But this roadside inn had no beds or even chairs. Actually, the inn was more like a barn with several large rooms and a trampled dirt floor. The toilet was outside behind a scraggly bush. But it didn't matter. I curled up next to Misha and Lena on a blanket Marusia had spread out and quickly fell asleep.

The next morning, Papa's brother Mitrofan and his wife, Maria, arrived. They had been living in Gulja for three months and were eagerly anticipating our arrival. The Shevchenkos and Dumanovskys came out to greet them with many hugs and tears.

"Where are Yakov and Pelageya?"

A moment of heavy silence followed Uncle Mitrofan's question.

"We buried Yakov near the border," Lueva said, "but we are hopeful that Pelageya is still alive. She got separated from our group just after we entered China."

"Then their children must come with us," Aunt Maria said, lifting me up as she spoke.

All four of us felt a huge relief when we heard these words. All of us liked our uncle and aunt. Uncle Mitrofan reminded me of Papa. He had that same jet-black hair, but unlike Papa, he had a wide mustache. I could see Papa's gentleness in his eyes. Aunt Maria was a short, well-built woman and was much more vocal than Uncle. She usually braided her long hair and twisted it into a bun, which she would cover with a pretty scarf.

Our aunt and uncle moved us into the two-room house they shared with two other families. Uncle Mitrofan and Aunt Maria slept on several layers of blankets in the rear right corner of our room. They made our bed on the concrete floor right next to theirs. Mama had packed a few warm blankets from Russia, and these became our bed and covering. Outside, our toilet was a hole in the ground straddled by several narrow planks. Going to the toilet on rainy nights was always a challenge.

The street we lived on had similar houses built very close one to another. Large metal gates and brick walls kept intruders and suspicious eyes out. The road outside our house was just wide enough for two horse-drawn wagons to pass. During the hot season, the dirt road turned into a dust bowl. When the rains came, it became a muddy mess. Along both sides of the road were narrow channels carrying sewage away from the homes. The stench was awful.

One week after arriving in Gulja, Uncle Mitrofan came home from his whitewashing job and told Marusia she was going somewhere else to live. He said a Muslim friend needed a nanny for his children, and Uncle had recommended Marusia for the job.

Misha had met some people who owned an apple orchard. They asked him to chase away the robins from their garden, not wanting them to eat their fruit. During the day, I would tag along with Misha as he "went to work." I would try to keep up with him as he would run, flailing his arms, through the garden. It was fun, plus Misha received some money and bread for his efforts.

Every Sunday morning we would wash up and prepare ourselves for church. Leaving the house early, we would walk several kilometers to a rented building that was our church. Close to one hundred adults and children attended these services.

Late at night, as I lay next to Misha and Lena, I would think about Mama, wondering where she was and whether I would ever see her again. We prayed with Uncle and Aunt every evening before we went to sleep, asking God to please bring Mama back to us.

One afternoon as Lena, Misha, and I were lying on our bed, we heard a commotion in the next room. Misha stood up and pressed his ear to the door.

"Be quiet, Vanya," he said. "Let's listen to what they are saying in the next room."

As we listened, suddenly Misha exclaimed, "That sounds like Mama's voice!"

I immediately jumped up and bolted for the door. Before I could reach it, Aunt Maria came in, blocking the way.

"Auntie, Auntie!" I screamed. "Mama has come back. I want to see her!" To my surprise, Aunt Maria grabbed me and pulled me away from the door.

"Quiet, children. Your mother did just come back. But I don't want you to go to her just yet. She doesn't know about your father's death, and she's too tired and weak to hear about that right now. She's already asked about you and Yakov, and we told her everything is alright. Let her rest a bit, and then I'll let you go to her."

As Aunt Maria placed me on the floor, I sat down next to Lena and Misha and began listening through the door to Mama telling the story of her three-week ordeal. Aunt Maria had left the door ajar so we could hear every word. Mama's voice sounded weak, like she had been sick, but it was the same sweet voice, and it gave me such comfort.

"When I returned to where my family and our group had been hiding, they were gone," Mama began. "I didn't know what to do, so I spent the night there, crying and praying for direction. In the morning I decided to leave and felt God leading me to walk in a certain direction. I had with me all the bread I had bought for my family.

"As I walked and prayed, I heard someone coming up behind me. It was a Muslim man riding a horse and pulling a bull carrying sacks of grain. The man stopped and asked in Kazakh, '*Kaida barashe, babeedia?*' (Where are you going, woman?)

"I had learned some Kazakh phrases back at the Sovxoz, and I greeted him and asked if this was the right direction to Gulja. He said yes and told me he could give me a ride as far as the mill. He was a kind man and let me ride his horse while he rode his overburdened bull.

"When we arrived at the mill, he showed me a road that he said led to a farm owned by some Russians. He said they could help me better because we spoke the same language. I thanked him for his help and walked on.

"Shortly after leaving the mill, I came to a fork in the road. The road he told me to take descended steeply down to a river. I waded into it, holding the bread high above my head and hoping the water wasn't too deep. But it was deep and fast, and I was swept off my feet. Several times I was pulled under the water by the current and almost drowned. It took all my strength to get to the other side. I lost all my bread, but at least I was alive.

"By the time I found the farm, I was shivering uncontrollably. I told the Russian family what had happened to me, and they quickly invited me into their home. They gave me dry clothes and let me warm myself next to their woodstove. But I still got very sick and had a high fever for several days. They told me I had malaria and that it could take weeks for me to get better.

"I stayed with this family for the next three weeks until my health returned. During that time, I knitted many socks, gloves, and blankets for these kind people. I couldn't wait to be strong enough to leave. I was very worried about my children and about Yakov.

"Early this morning, the owner of the farm said he would be traveling to a village near Gulja, and I persuaded him to take me along. When we arrived there, he paid for a horse-drawn wagon to bring me here to Gulja. Bless God, I finally made it!"

We heard murmurs of thanksgiving from Uncle Mitrofan and Aunt Maria, who had returned to the room. And then, an uncomfortable silence.

"You're sure Yakov and my children are okay? Where is Yakov?"

"They're fine, Pelageya, they are all resting. Now please try to rest. You're still not well, and you look exhausted."

I couldn't tell who had said that, but I knew they were just trying to shield Mama from being shocked by Papa's death.

"By the way," the same voice asked, "what happened to your legs?"

"Oh, they're much better now," Mama replied. "I lost my shoes in the river and walked for many kilometers barefooted. I also bruised and scraped my legs against large rocks in the river."

I wanted to run to Mama and tell her all about Papa and about our trip to Gulja. But when I looked over at Misha, he motioned for me to stay put. I heard somebody else enter the room, and as the woman began speaking, Misha gasped, "Oh, my God, no!"

"Da, Pelageya," the woman said. "You buried your son Vasya in the sand, and then without you they buried your Yakuba."

"What!" Mama shouted.

"Yes, your Yakov is dead. The same night you sat waiting, they buried him."

Mama began wailing an awful, mournful sound that sent shivers through Misha, Lena, and me. "Is this true?" she shrieked. "Am I left all alone with four little children? O Lord, what am I to do? We don't speak the language. We have no money. Oh, oh, oh!"

"Why did you do that?" Aunt Maria yelled at the woman. "After all the hardships she went through. What's the matter with you? Couldn't you wait to tell her later? Now look at what you've done."

Misha sprang to his feet and burst through the door. Lena and I followed him as fast as we could. Mama was groaning loudly, and someone said paralysis was setting in. The men were placing Mama on a bed of hay when we ran up to her.

"Mama! Mama!" Misha threw his arms around her, and both began sobbing.

When Mama saw Lena and me, she tried to lift us up but couldn't. Someone picked us up, and we, too, snuggled into our mama's arms. Tears of both joy and sorrow gushed down my cheeks. I was so happy to see Mama but horrified at how sick she looked.

Mama kept squeezing my head against her bosom and murmuring questions to God. "What now, Lord? Yakov is dead and my children are so small. Oh, oh . . ."

"It will be alright, Pelageya," Uncle Mitrofan said. "God isn't without mercy. He hasn't forsaken you. We'll help you, and so will others."

Mama nodded weakly. "Where is Marusia?" she whispered, but before we could respond, she fell into a deep sleep.

MAMA NEVER DID recover from the shock of that awful night. For the next six months she stayed in bed. She had malarial attacks twice a day, raging fevers, and chills that shook her without mercy. Every day Misha would gather sticks for the stove and Marusia, who came home every evening, would make hot tea for Mama. People brought food for us and helped all they could, which wasn't much, because they were also poor and had their own families to feed. Misha and I also came down with malaria, but we determined that if any of us were to survive, we had to find food for our family.

One cold morning we awoke hungry and again had no food. Misha saw my pained expression and said, "Vanya, we have to find some bread for Mama and ourselves. Let me teach you some Kazakh phrases and show you how to beg for food. I'm much too old and embarrassed to beg myself, but I can teach you how to do it."

"Okay," I said. "When do we start?"

Misha taught me one phrase and had me repeat it until I said it like a native Kazakh.

"Nan bearch, nan bearch, nan bearch." Over and over I said it.

"What exactly does it mean?"

"It means 'Give me bread,'" Misha said.

Misha would lead me into a doorway, knock on the door, and hide. As the door swung open, I would look up and say, "Nan bearch."

I would extend my right hand toward the person and repeat my phrase. Maybe because of my dirty clothes or because I was so small and skinny, most people gave me pieces of round flat bread, which I dropped into a well-used cloth bag.

Many times people would give us bread covered with what looked like shiny green hair. For some reason, every time I ate this bread, I would have a terrible stomachache all night. Sadly, almost half of all the bread we were given looked like this.

Begging was not easy, though. Once, as we turned into a doorway, we were met by two scraggly looking black dogs. Before we could get away, the dogs charged us and began biting our legs and arms. I screamed and flailed my arms, and Misha had to drag me away. Both of us were bleeding badly from bite wounds when Misha led us to the safety of an abandoned shed. In his back pocket he had a dirty rag. He wet the rag in a water puddle and began carefully wiping my wounds.

"I lost the bag of bread," I said, tears running down my cheeks.

"That's alright, Vanya. We'll find another bag and get more bread."

Every day right at noontime, I would have a malaria attack. Misha would lead me behind some building, strip off his jacket, cover me with it, and sit on top of me. I would shake violently for at least ten minutes and then break into profuse sweating. Misha would then lie on me for at least thirty minutes, trying to keep me warm. After an hour or so, we would get up and continue begging for bread.

Misha's malaria attacks always occurred at night when we were already at home.

One afternoon, after Misha had gone to the bazaar to buy salt, Mama called Marusia, Lena, and me to her bedside. She was whimpering, and I could barely hear what she was saying.

"Give me your hands, children. I love you so very much. Oh, Yakov, what should I do? Should I go to you or stay with my children?"

Mama sighed deeply, closed her eyes, and slumped her head to one side. Misha walked in at that point and said, "Is Mama okay?"

Marusia looked up and with tears trickling down her cheeks said, "No, Misha. Mama is dead."

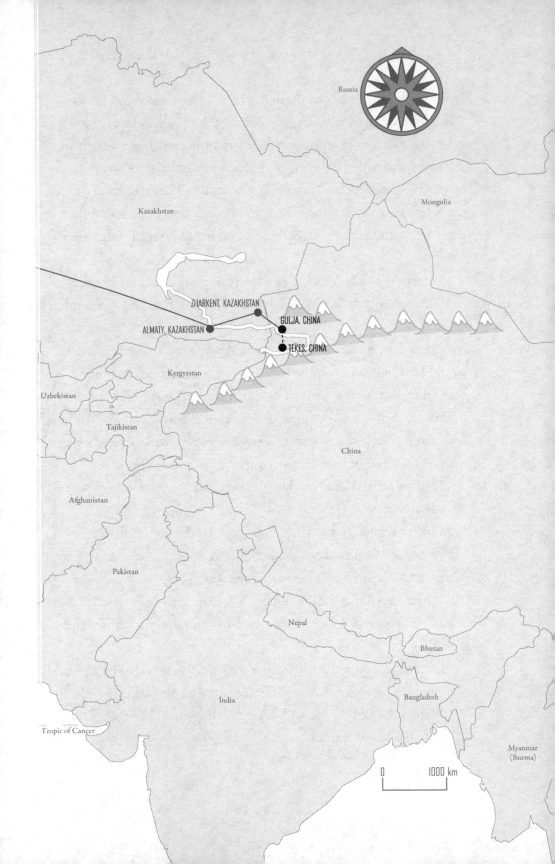

FOUR

MAMA LOOKED SO PEACEFUL now, but what little peace
and stability there was for us Iliyn children shattered in
that horrible moment. Misha flung himself across Mama's
body, which was turning gray and cold.

"No, Mama, don't go! Mama, Mama, why did you have to die?"

All four of us were screaming and crying. Nobody else was in that
shabby little room we had all shared. Uncle Mitrofan and Aunt Maria
had left it to us a few weeks earlier when they moved south to find
work. I kept holding Mama's hand, stroking her bony fingers. Misha
and Marusia were lying on top of Mama, hugging her and wailing.
Lena sat next to Mama's feet, sobbing and beating the ground with
her fists.

Thailand

Philippines

Our Kazakh neighbors must have heard us, because they ran into the room without knocking. The father came up to Mama, felt her pulse, and said something in Kazakh to his wife. They began pulling us away from Mama and sat us on the floor in the opposite corner.

Within minutes, our little room filled with people. Mrs. Shevchenko sat with us, trying to quiet us down. Her son Alex, along with several other young men, left to find some boards. I overheard them say they needed to build a coffin for Mama.

By the time they returned, Mama had been all washed up by the women from our church. The women lovingly dressed Mama in her only white blouse and tied a scarf underneath her chin. Then they placed her frail body into a coffin made of discarded wood, probably from the side of a barn or some other crumbling building.

I watched this happening, but it seemed like just a bad dream. How could this be real? Just two hours ago I was talking to Mama. Now she was in that awful box. When Mrs. Shevchenko led us outside, it seemed like the whole church had gathered there. Alex and some other men carried out Mama's coffin and placed it onto an old farm wagon. Lena and I were lifted up and sat next to the driver. As the horses began walking, all the people followed along. They sang a Russian hymn as we wound through town to a cemetery on the outskirts of Gulja.

The wagon stopped next to a large hole, and Mama's coffin was placed on the ground. People came up and touched my shoulder, but I could barely focus through my tears. I heard several of the men read from the Bible and say kind things about Mama. I just kept staring at the coffin, which was still open. Even though I knew Mama had died, it didn't hit me until her coffin was closed and they had begun lowering it into the big hole. I began screaming, "No! Don't put Mama in there!"

I ran up to the grave and tried to jump down onto the coffin to be with Mama. Alex grabbed me and held me tightly.

"Mama, don't go!" I cried, reaching my hand out to her.

All the women were weeping openly, and most of the men had tears in their eyes. Misha, Marusia, and Lena ran up and embraced me. We stood for a long time like that, clinging to each other, weeping and watching Mama's grave fill up with dirt. We were four orphaned children with a future as uncertain as the swirling desert winds of this strange new country.

Were it not for the Shevchenkos' kindness, the confusion and pain and loneliness of those following weeks would have surely overwhelmed us Iliyn children. We moved in with the Shevchenkos, who became our family. Efrem and his wife, Niuta, cared for us like their own children, even though they were as poor as everybody else. They had five children of their own, including my friend Alex. Alex's sunken eyes and weather-beaten face made him look older than his seventeen years, but he had a kindly smile that had warmed my spirit from the time I first met him back in Zharkent. He had helped Papa a lot during our trek into China, and he began looking out for us after Papa died.

Misha began looking for work but couldn't find anyone willing to hire a skinny Russian boy. Marusia continued to live with the Muslim family and serve as nanny to their children. Misha and I kept walking the streets and begging for food, since there never seemed to be enough to eat. Often we would visit Marusia's home, and the Kazakh family would give us moldy bread to eat. We never minded the green-spotted bread. We ate each bite. Better to have old bread than no bread. Many nights we went to sleep with aching, empty stomachs.

We lived with the Shevchenkos for several weeks before they found other homes for us. Misha and Marusia were taken in by the

Tatejnin family. Lena was taken in by a teacher who lived far away in Urümqi. I was left all alone for several more days before I got a new family.

ONE DAY, a man named Igor Grusha and his wife, Lyuda, visited the Shevchenkos because they had heard that an orphan boy needed a home. The Grushas had lived in Gulja for many years, having moved from Russia when the Soviet government promised them farmland. They seemed to be decent people, although they were not Christian.

At first, the Shevchenkos were hesitant to let me live with a non-Christian family, but the Grushas promised to take good care of me, as they were better off financially than most people in town. I guess they were successful farmers. After a tearful goodbye with Alex and his family, I hopped on the Grushas' wagon and headed for my new home.

The first thing I noticed about the Grushas' home was the good number of pear trees in front of the house. A few overripe pears had fallen on the ground and were starting to decay.

"Do you like pears?" Igor asked.

"Well, yes," I replied.

"Good. Then that's one of the chores I'll give you—to pick them and get rid of the ones that are on the ground."

"Okay," I said.

The Grushas had seemed much friendlier when they were at the Shevchenkos, but now I noticed that they didn't smile as much. And their house didn't seem as nice as I had thought it would be, compared to how they had described it. We walked in, and Lyuda took my belongings to a small back room where they stored big glass jars.

"You can sleep here," Lyuda said, pointing to a stack of blankets in a corner of the room. The room had a little window looking out into their pear orchard. I was happy to have my own little space, even if I had to share it with a bunch of jars.

Before I went to sleep that first night in my new home, I thanked God for my new family and prayed that they would like me. I was scared and excited at the same time. It was nice to have a family, but I couldn't believe they didn't believe in God. No one came in to pray with me before bed. This made me miss the nights that Papa would tuck me into bed and pray with me. That had always made me feel so secure.

The next day, Lyuda gave me some chores to do. After helping her clean the kitchen, I went outside to collect the rotting pears. What a shame, I thought, that all these pears were going to waste. How my sisters and Misha and I would have loved to have eaten them when we were traveling. To think that I was hungry all those times, and here I was, surrounded by food. I wanted to eat a pear, but I was unsure whether Igor and Lyuda would get mad at me if I did.

Throughout the day, all kinds of men came by my new house. Some were Muslim, dark-skinned men, and others were Russian, their faces reddened by the sun.

When I went inside after picking up the pears, I noticed a funny smell. I saw Igor and two other men drinking something out of a bottle, smoking cigarettes, and eating bread and cabbage. They were laughing and shouting at each other in words I had never heard before. Just as I was about to go into my room, Igor shouted, "Vanya, come here, son! This is my new boy! He's going to be happy here, aren't you, boy?"

The men roared with laughter. I tried to smile, but I couldn't help wondering about the awful smell that was coming from their mouths. One of the men, probably a Kazakh, brought his face close to mine and asked, "You like to drink?"

I didn't know what to say, and his breath smelled really bad.

"Shut up!" Igor said to the man as he grabbed me away. "He's too young yet. I invited him here so you can see what a nice son we've adopted, not one to be corrupted by your poor character."

Everyone started laughing again. As I left the room, I couldn't understand what had been so funny. All I knew was that I had never been around people who acted like that. It was almost as if they were crazy. I hadn't thought that Igor was strange the first time I met him.

That night, as I lay in bed talking to God and praying that my brother and sisters were all right, I started to cry. I missed my papa and my mama and Misha, Marusia, and Lena. It seemed like my family was gone. I wondered what it would be like to live with the Grushas from now on.

It was the middle of the night, and I hadn't been able to fall asleep. The men's laughter still rang in my ears. The men didn't seem to be happy, but why did they laugh so much? Then all of a sudden I heard a tap on my window.

"Vanya!"

Who could this be? I wondered.

"Vanya, are you in there?" someone whispered.

"Who is that?" I whispered back. I got up to look out my window. It was Misha.

"Misha! What are you doing here?"

"Shhh! Don't talk anymore," Misha said. "Go grab your clothes and come with me. Alex and his dad are out by the road, and we've come to get you."

"Wh . . . why?" I stammered, getting my clothes and putting them in my arms.

"Don't ask. I'll tell you when we get in the wagon. Hurry!"

With that, I tried to be as quiet as possible and walked out the front door, closing it carefully behind me. Misha ran to the road, dragging me behind him. The Shevchenkos motioned for me to get into the wagon.

"Vanya, I didn't realize this, but I almost gave you away to bad people!" Alex's dad, Efrem, said. "After you had gone with the Grushas, someone in the marketplace told me that they are famous for selling vodka and other kinds of alcohol. They couldn't believe that we had given you over to them, and we decided to kidnap you back. Forgive me, Vanya. From now on, we will only let you live with believers."

I couldn't believe my ears. I remember Papa telling me that alcohol and vodka were very bad and that people who drank it regularly were addicted to it. He also told me it was something that made people lose their minds. So I guess that's what that smell was. Those men sure had acted strangely.

Efrem, Alex, and Misha seemed nervous as we got closer and closer to the Shevchenkos' home. They kept looking back, as though they were expecting someone to be following us.

"Why do you keep glancing back?" I asked.

"If the Grushas find out we kidnapped you, they might try to take you back," Misha said. "We need to get you far away from Gulja as soon as we can."

When we arrived at the Shevchenkos' home, a wagon with two sweaty horses was standing next to the front door. As I jumped out of our wagon, a man walked out the front door and approached us. I lifted my head to gaze into his face, and I heard Misha say, "Vanya, meet your new papa."

"Hello, Vanya. My name is Ivan Verhovod."

Misha suddenly grabbed me by the shoulders and dragged me off to the side. He looked deep into my eyes and said, "You need to leave with Ivan tonight, before the Grushas find out we took you."

"But who is Ivan?" I asked. "And what do I call him?"

Misha explained that Ivan had helped lead our group into China. He now lived with his wife, Masha, in Tekes, a town in the mountains two hundred kilometers south of Gulja. Since they had no children, Masha had sent her husband to Gulja with instructions to find her a little orphan girl who could help with domestic chores around their farm. When Ivan arrived in Gulja, the Shevchenkos told him that I was the only orphan left without a home. Mr. Verhovod, being a kind and gentle man, didn't think his wife would mind it if he brought me home instead of a girl. So he agreed to take me.

"I know it will be difficult for you to call him Papa right away," Misha added, "because our real papa is in heaven. But can you try?"

"Vanya, we must leave."

As I glanced toward my new papa who was waving his hand frantically, tears suddenly filled my eyes.

"Misha!" I cried. "I don't want to leave you."

As Misha hugged me, I could feel his warm tears on my head and nose. Misha, sobbing loudly and pushing me toward the wagon, said, "Vanyushka, I love you. I don't know how, but I will see you again. Go with God, little brother."

I cried openly as I parted with Misha and the Shevchenkos, my first family since becoming an orphan. I desperately wanted a good home and to not be hungry anymore. But as we rode out of Gulja, I wondered whether I would ever see my brother and sisters again. Would I ever again see any of the friends who had helped our family escape from Russia?

PART 2

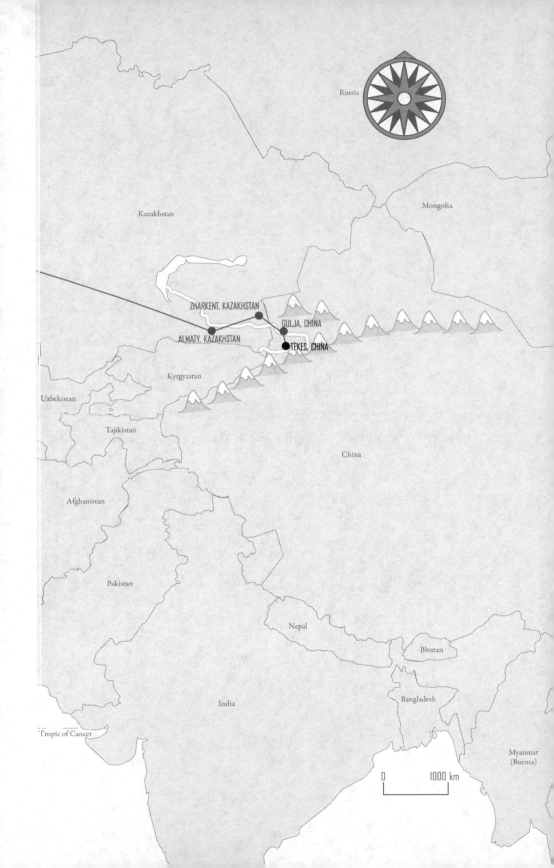

Russia

Mongolia

Kazakhstan

ZHARKENT, KAZAKHSTAN

GULJA, CHINA

ALMATY, KAZAKHSTAN

TEKES, CHINA

Kyrgyzstan

Uzbekistan

Tajikistan

China

Afghanistan

Pakistan

Nepal

Bhutan

Bangladesh

India

Tropic of Cancer

Myanmar
(Burma)

0   1000 km

T HE TRIP TO TEKES in the fall of 1933 had taken us five days and nights of hard travel. Our wagon was pulled by two horses and was filled with supplies purchased in Gulja. I quickly began calling Mr. Verhovod Papa, since he treated me just like a son. Papa was kind to me and even let me hold the reins a few times. We stopped several times along the way and slept under the open sky.

The Verhovods' weathered, wood-frame house was in the tiny farming village of Chicaredi. As we pulled into the front yard of my new home, I saw Ivan Verhovod's wife, Masha, standing in the doorway, staring at me. *Something must be wrong,* I thought. She didn't look happy at all.

Thailand

Philippines

Happy she wasn't! As I got down from the wagon, my new mama stared at me with cold eyes and then, turning to Papa, said with disgust in her voice, "What's this? Why did you bring me this dog? I told you I wanted a little girl. I don't need him. Look at him. He looks like a scraggly little dog. He'll probably remain a mutt till he becomes an old man. I can't believe you brought him! What do we do with him? He'll just be an extra mouth to feed."

Masha came up and yanked at my ear. The look on her face was terrifying.

"He smells like a dog!" she said, pushing me to the ground.

I had such hopes that my new mama would treat me as kindly as my own mother had, but now I was shaking with fear as Masha Verhovod stood over me, seething with anger. Papa came and lifted me up, placing his hand on my shoulder.

"Masha," he said, "there were no little girls left. Vanya was the only orphan without a home. What was I supposed to do?"

"You should have left him in Gulja," Masha said as she stormed back into the house. Papa looked puzzled and a little unsure of himself. He patted me on my head and said, "Don't worry, Vanya. I'm sure things will work out. Come on and help me unload the wagon."

As we unloaded the wagon, I kept noticing Masha staring at me through the window. When we had finished, Papa led me over to a pail of water and helped me wash my face and hands. It was almost dinnertime as I walked into my new home for the first time.

With my hands at my side and staring at the floor, I waited to be told what to do. Masha ignored me as she went about her business. Papa walked up to me and pushed me in the direction of a small table. There were only two chairs, and turning to Masha, Papa said, "Where's Vanya supposed to sit?"

"Over there in the corner," she replied, pointing behind Papa's chair.

I shuffled over to the corner and slid down. Masha shoved a small plate of potatoes and some chicken skin over to me. Masha and Papa sat down to eat.

That night I pleaded with God, "Please make my new mama like me."

I guess we just don't get the answer we want to some prayers, because Masha never did like me, though I started calling her Mama by the second day. I think she despised me. I know she wanted a girl, but I tried so hard to make her like me. I did everything she told me to do, but it never seemed enough.

Mama had a look that could kill. Whenever she slightly bowed her head and looked at me, with her brow furrowed and her nostrils flared, I immediatcly winced, knowing a beating was coming. I usually didn't even know what I had done wrong, but somehow Mama had become angry at me. Inside the broom closet Mama kept a leather belt that was reserved just for me. Every time she reached for that closet, I would shut my eyes and clench my fists in anticipation of the blows.

Rarely did I deserve the beating. It was usually something that just made Mama angry, like the time I spilled my milk. I could never forget that horrible day. In the morning, Mama had told me to help with the wheat and barley harvest. Papa and I worked in the field all day. What made the work especially hard for me was that I had no shoes. I had outgrown mine since arriving here, and Mama never bought me a new pair. By the end of the day, the soles of my feet and my legs were bloody from stepping on rocks and scraping up against the wheat and barley stocks.

By sunset, we were both famished. Papa helped me wash my hands and face and wiped my bloody legs with a damp cloth. As we walked into the house, Mama was placing dinner on the table. She had since allowed me to sit at the table, although my chair was so low that my chin barely reached the table.

Papa prayed for the meal, and we began to eat. Mama had made *vareniki* (potato dumplings) and plopped two of them on my plate. Next to Papa was a stack of fresh bread covered with thick pieces of butter.

"Papa, would you please hand me a piece of bread?" I asked.

Mama reached over for the bread, broke off a small piece and knocked the butter off before passing it on to me.

Papa looked at Mama and asked, "Masha, why did you knock the butter off?"

"What does he need butter for?" Mama said. "Besides, we'll have more to sell."

Looking at me, Mama said, "Here's a glass of milk, Vanya."

I gladly took the glass, knowing full well that she wasn't giving me the kind of milk she and Papa drank. I had seen Mama many times use the separator to make butter. Mama was giving me whatever was left after making butter and cream. It didn't look like the milk Papa and Mama drank. My milk was watery and tasted strange.

After taking a sip, I reached up to place my glass next to my dish but accidentally hit the edge of the table. The milk spilled into my plate and onto the table, running off right into Mama's lap.

"Why, you little dog!" Mama screamed as she pushed herself away from the table. She had that terrible look on her face as she walked over to me.

"What's the matter with you? Can't you even drink properly?"

She grabbed my ear and yanked me off my chair.

"Masha, don't spank him. It was an accident," Papa said.

"I told you he was worthless the day you brought him into our house. I'll teach him yet!"

Mama was hysterical by now and was dragging me over to the broom closet. My ear felt like it was going to be torn right off. Out came that dreaded leather belt, and Mama started whipping me all over. She held onto my ear as she beat me on my legs, my bottom, and my back. Some of the wounds on my legs opened up and began to bleed. That made Mama even madder. I wanted to scream but knew that would only make Mama beat me more, so I moaned and wept inside.

"Get on your knees and stay in that corner!" Mama yelled.

At last the beating was over, and I crawled over to the corner.

I could hear Papa pleading with Mama. "Mashenka, why do you treat Vanya this way? He's just a little boy."

"I don't like him," Mama fumed. "He's always getting in the way, and he's so tiny and skinny. I told you I wanted a girl."

As they argued, I reached up to touch my ear and winced from the pain. It felt as if my earlobe had torn away from my head. Dropping my hand back into my lap, I spied blood on my thumb. My legs were still bleeding, and my back was smarting. But my real pain was inside, in my heart.

I stayed in that corner till Papa and Mama had finished dinner. Mama sent me to bed hungry.

"Next time," she said, "you'll not be so unruly at the dinner table. Now carry out the trash and get to bed."

I looked forward to crawling into bed because I felt safe there. I could dream of my real papa and mama, of Misha, Marusia, and

Lena. How I missed them! I would dream of Mama tucking me into bed and of Papa telling us Bible stories. I dreamed of begging for bread with Misha, which seemed like paradise compared to my present life. Often I would wake up in the night crying and calling out for Papa and Mama.

I also had dreams about corners. Because Mama beat me so often and usually for no reason, I developed a fondness for dark, out-of-the-way corners where I could be all on my own, where Mama could not find me and beat me. In my dreams I spoke to these corners like they were my friends, and they covered me like a warm blanket on a cold night.

Mama didn't like me to pray alone in my little corners. Once, after another beating, I crawled outside and leaned against the outhouse. Nobody was around, so I began to pour out my hurts to God.

"Dearest Father, please take me to heaven. Papa and Mama told me they would be waiting for me in heaven, and I want to be with them right now. My new mama doesn't like me, and I'm terribly afraid of her. She beats me for no reason at all, screaming into my ear that I'm a dog. Why does she call me a dog? Papa and Mama never called me a dog.

"No one understands me, God. Papa is nice, but he never stops Mama from beating me. I can't run to Misha. He lives too far away. You're the only One I can talk to. Papa always told me that no matter what happens, I could always depend on You. I hope You can hear me now."

Suddenly the door flew open and Mama stormed out. As I sheepishly looked up at Mama, her nostrils flared as she yelled, "Oh, so you're unhappy with us, are you? I'll teach you to be more grateful!" Once again, she used that leather belt liberally on my back.

Dotia, our next-door neighbor and Mama's younger sister, saw the way she beat me. Dotia was a kind woman and often scolded Mama. "Masha," she would say, "you're going to have to answer to God for the way you're abusing this orphaned boy."

Masha would sneer at her. "If you don't like the way I treat him, why don't you take him and raise him yourself?"

Finding a quiet, dark corner became my secret game. It was difficult because our house was so little, but I found many places outside where no one, especially Mama, would see me crying and talking to the only One who understood me, God.

One year after moving in with the Verhovods, Papa said we were moving to another village called Karasuijka. Mama's sister Dotia was not moving with us. Papa said another family, the Demchenkos, would move with us.

Our new home was a two-room house separated by a hallway. Out back was an old barn and enough land for a good-sized garden. We lived in one room, and the Demchenkos lived in the other. Mama quickly got the house in shape while Papa and I helped Soviestej Demchenko get the barn fixed up to hold chickens and cows.

During the next few weeks, we were so busy getting the house fixed up that Mama didn't have time to worry about me or beat me. Papa and Soviestej worked on fixing broken fences while Mama and Dooshaijka Demchenko outfitted the barn for their laying hens. Each woman had twenty-five hens.

One morning as I sat at the breakfast table, Mama surprised me with a new red shirt she had sewn just for me. It was the first piece of new clothing I had received since arriving over a year ago.

"Now you make sure to take care of this shirt," Mama said. "I spent a lot of time sewing it for you."

As I clutched it to my chest, I said, "Thank you, Mama. I'll be sure to take good care of it."

Several weeks later, I was wearing my red shirt while working out in the yard. Mama and Papa had gone for the day to another village and left me in charge of the animals. I was almost seven years old, and I didn't want to disappoint Mama.

Papa had five cows and one young bull. While herding the cows into their holding pen, the bull suddenly knocked me over on my back. Before I could get up, he walked up to me and stood right over me. I knew if he shifted his hooves just a few inches either way, he would crush my stomach.

I began crying and yelling for help. Fortunately, Dooshaijka was home and heard me. She ran up to the bull and shooed him away.

"Did he hurt you?" she asked.

"I don't think so."

"Then why are you crying?"

I showed her the tear in my red shirt. "When Mama sees this tear, she's going to beat me."

"Take your shirt off," she said. "I'll sew it up so that Masha can't see the tear right away, and then I'll convince her not to beat you."

Dooshaijka helped me like this many other times. She was as kind to me as Dotia had been in the old house.

Masha and Dooshaijka were opposites when it came to the way they ran their homes. Masha was not anywhere as organized as Dooshaijka. Take, for instance, their chickens. Dooshaijka had cages built for her hens, and because of the cages she never lost an egg. Masha, on the other hand, let her hens run all over the place. Often her hens laid eggs under bushes or stacks of hay.

One of my daily morning chores was to collect these eggs and bring them to Mama. Mama would usually feel her hens the night before and tell me at dinnertime how many eggs I was to find the next day. In the morning, I would lift the hens and carefully collect their eggs, trying not to crack or drop them. Collecting the eggs was not my main problem. Finding the eggs was.

Whenever I couldn't find all the eggs, I dreaded walking into the house. With my hands full of eggs, I would open the back door with my leg and come into the kitchen. Mama would turn to me and ask, "Did you find all twenty eggs?"

Looking down at the floor, I'd say, "No, Mama. I could only find eighteen eggs. I looked everywhere, Mama, but I couldn't find the other two eggs."

By now Mama was facing me with her hands on her hips. "You good-for-nothing boy!" she'd say. "Lost my eggs again, did you? Give me the eggs."

One time, Mama yanked my ear, forcing me onto my knees. Out of the broom closet came the dreaded leather strap, and Mama beat me for not finding all twenty eggs.

After I'd been on my knees for a long time, Mama finally told me to continue my chores. I ran out the back door and flew into the barn. With my back still smarting from the blows, I fled to my special corner. I needed to hide from people for a while and talk to my only true Friend, to my Father God.

My special corner was in the back of the barn next to piles of cow manure. I knew that Papa rarely came back there, so I could be alone for a little while. Falling to my knees, I covered my face with my hands and called out to God.

"Dear Father, why does my mama hate me so much? I really do

try to obey her, but she never seems to notice. You know it wasn't my fault that I couldn't find twenty eggs. My real mama never used to beat me like this. Could you tell Mama and Papa I love them and I really miss them? Maybe you could just take me home right now."

I couldn't contain my tears.

This scene soon became a daily routine for me. I hated mornings almost as much as I hated chickens. Why couldn't they just lay their eggs where they were supposed to!

One evening, Mama told me that twenty-two hens were with eggs. The next morning I prayed as I inspected each hen. "Oh, please be there!"

After making sure I had found every egg there was, I counted them. To my shock, I counted only nineteen eggs. I searched frantically for the other three eggs but to no avail. Tears started flowing even before I had gathered the eggs in my arms. I could almost feel the blows on my back.

Stepping out of the barn, I couldn't even see the back door because of my tears. Slowly and with much hesitation, I started walking toward the kitchen.

"Vanya, why are you crying? What's the matter?"

The question startled me, causing me to almost drop the eggs. As I looked up, I was pleased to see Dooshaijka.

"I . . . I . . . found only nineteen eggs, and Mama is going to beat me," I stammered, barely able to speak.

"How many eggs were you supposed to find?" she asked.

"Twenty-two."

Dooshaijka quickly took me by my arm and led me back inside the barn. She opened three of her cages, took out three eggs, and handed them to me.

"Here," she said. "Masha will never know I gave these to you. Now run along."

"Tha . . . thank you," I said, and for the first time that morning, a smile appeared on my face. I could scarcely believe how blessed I was to have such a kind neighbor as Dooshaijka. As I walked toward our back door, I felt a sense of goodness overwhelm me. Somebody cared enough for me to actually help me.

Mama didn't beat me that morning because of Dooshaijka. And that was not the last time Dooshaijka helped me. During the four-plus years I lived in that house, Dooshaijka helped me so many times I lost count. Every time I couldn't find all the eggs, I would pray, "Please, dear God, let Dooshaijka be home, and let her be looking out the window."

Dooshaijka was like a beautiful rose in the midst of a dry desert. My times alone were often spent in prayer for Dooshaijka and thanking God for sending someone to care for me.

One evening as we were eating dinner, Papa turned to me and said, "Vanya, Masha and I will be leaving for Gulja tomorrow, and we'll be gone for five months. You're nine years old now and should be able to take care of yourself. Masha's sister Nastia has agreed to let you live with her family while we're gone. They live near Tekes, which is on the way to Gulja. You need to be ready to leave early tomorrow."

I was startled to hear this. Was this good news or bad? I knew Nastia had four children of her own, and maybe she would be a lot kinder to me than Mama. But it was hard for me to imagine living with someone who wouldn't beat me.

Looking at me sternly, Mama added, "We will be leaving you in charge of our twelve head of cattle, and you had better take good care of them. I told Nastia that you can herd their cattle along with ours. They have forty-two head of cattle. If I hear something happened to our cattle or to Nastia's, you will be in big trouble. Do you understand?"

"Ye . . . ye . . . yes, Mama," I stammered, barely able to respond to her stern words.

Fifty-four head of cattle! I thought. *I've never herded that many cows before. I wonder what it's going to be like.*

I had mixed emotions the next morning as we were leaving. Terrible as these four years had been, this had been my home. As I herded the cows behind Papa's wagon, I glanced back at the barn. I sure wasn't going to miss those noisy chickens! But I would miss my secret corner, that place where I had spent so much of my free time talking to my Friend and Father. Wherever I lived, I'd have to find another special corner like that.

Dooshaijka came out with her husband to say goodbye. I wanted to run up and hug her, but I was afraid of Mama's reaction. Dooshaijka knelt and whispered in my ear as she hugged me. "I'm going to miss you, Vanya. You're a good boy, and I know God is going to make something out of you. I'll be praying for you."

As she began to stand up, I threw my arms around her neck and hugged her. With tears in my eyes, I whispered in her ear, "Thank you so much for all those eggs you gave me. I'll never forget your kindness to me."

I felt a sharp pain on the side of my head as Mama ripped at my ear.

"That's enough, Vanya. Get into the wagon."

Looking at Dooshaijka, Mama said, "We'll be back in five months. Make sure our house and animals are taken care of. Goodbye."

Even though Mama told Dooshaijka we would be back in five months, I wondered whether I would ever see this place again. As the wagon started moving, I stole one last look and, barely moving my hand, waved goodbye to the Demchenkos, to my corner, and to Mama's miserable chickens.

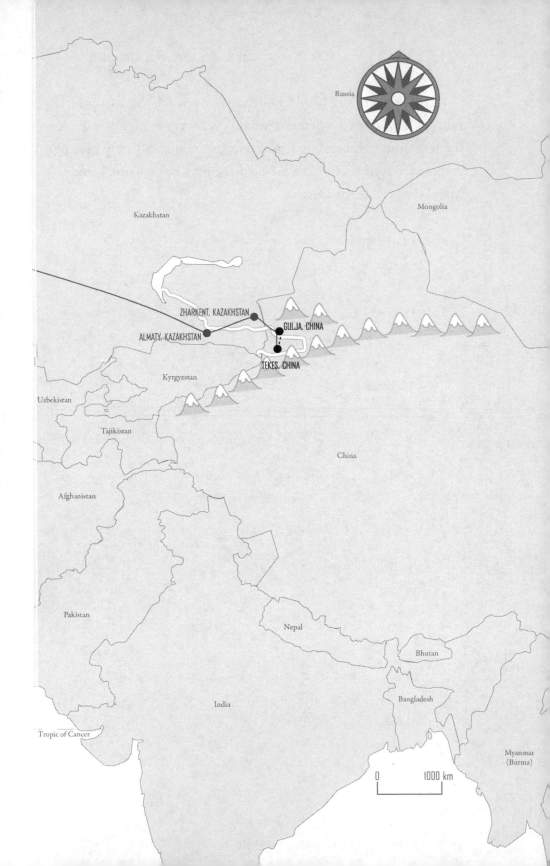

SIX

NASTIA, HER HUSBAND VICTOR, and their four small children lived on a wheat farm nestled in the shadow of the snow-covered Tien Shan Mountains outside Tekes. Their house was much bigger than Ivan and Masha's, and Victor had several hired men working on their farm. I slept in a small room along with three older workers. I noticed that all the others had shoes, but nobody seemed to care that I worked barefoot.

Nastia was very good to me, never mistreating or spanking me. She gave me a jacket to wear during the cold spring mornings, and I never went hungry. Shortly after I arrived, Victor took me out to their field and showed me the cattle. Together with Papa's cows, there were fifty-four head of cattle. I had never before seen so many cows in one place and was afraid I couldn't handle them all. But Victor was a patient teacher, and during my first week he taught me all I needed to know about how to care for them.

Early one spring morning, as I herded the cattle out to pasture, the sky turned black with angry-looking clouds, and it began to rain. I was wearing the jacket Nastia had given me, but I still shivered from the freezing rain. Then the weather quickly changed from rain to hail. My jacket was soaked, and after a short while I couldn't feel my feet. Everything around me turned white—everything except my bare feet, which were turning blue from the cold. Several times as I ran after stray cattle, I slipped and fell facedown on the icy ground.

I quickly herded the cattle under a grove of trees and huddled next to several calves, trying to get warm. I even shoved my frost-bitten feet into fresh cow dung to try to get some feeling into my toes. When the storm passed, I pushed the cows toward home, feeling stabs of pain with every step. I had never felt so cold in my life. When I finally spotted the farm off in the distance, I started to cry. Nastia welcomed me home and bandaged my bleeding feet, but I felt so helpless and cold.

When summer came, the weather in Tekes turned blazing hot. With little or no rain, the grass dried up and our cattle needed to be constantly herded to new pastures and water sources. By six in the morning each day I would be on my way, some days walking over fifteen kilometers till I found suitable pasture and water for the cows. I usually tried herding the cows along the roadside, but often they wandered into other fields, provoking angry outbursts from the local wheat farmers.

During the first weeks, herding the cows to higher pastures was exciting. I enjoyed being out in the open field all day by myself, with nobody to beat me and make fun of me. Just me, my cows, and God's creation. It was like one great big corner of God's world set apart just for me. I actually stopped looking over my shoulder, convinced at last that Mama was gone and, at least for now, would not beat me or yank my ear.

It was during those long days out in the open fields that I wished someone had taught me to read. Mama never sent me to school. She said I would be as dumb as a dog all my life and there wasn't any reason to waste someone's time trying to teach me to read. But I knew I could learn to read if given the chance.

In my daydreams I thought of the Bible stories Papa had read to us years ago. It seemed like a long time ago, but the stories were still fresh in my mind. I really liked the story about David, the shepherd. *Kind of reminds me of what I'm doing, except David had to protect his sheep against lions and bears.*

I'd never seen a lion or a bear and wondered what I'd do if one attacked our cows. Then I thought of young David fighting the giant Goliath with a slingshot. I especially liked the part of the story where David kills Goliath and cuts his head off. I was quite sure I would be brave, too, if I owned a slingshot.

If I had to herd the cows far away from home, I sometimes had to sleep out in the field with them. I never went to sleep hungry like before. Nastia always gave me ample supplies of fresh bread and a sour milk drink called *ayran.* But I often went to sleep aching from loneliness. Sometimes for one week I wouldn't see another human being—just cows, heat, dust, and flies. As the summer heat intensified, I began to despise the irritating black flies and the huge clouds of dust kicked up by the cows every time I had to move them. My eyes would get terribly irritated by the dust and by my constant rubbing. Every day it grew more miserable and boring and lonely.

I detested these cows and this awful job. I would easily trade this job for some other kind of work, but I knew there was no way Victor and Nastia would release me. Mama had told them I would herd their cows till they got back. The only thing I could do was talk to God.

Every evening after herding the cows under some protection, I would drop to my knees and pray. "Dear Father, thank you for Victor and Nastia. They have been kind to me. Nastia gives me more food than Mama ever did, and she has never beaten me. Victor reminds me of Papa; he's kind and helpful. It's these cows that I hate. Is this all that I'm going to do for the rest of my life? I want to learn to read and then maybe learn to make and repair shoes, just like Papa."

As time went on, my prayers got bolder and louder. I would fall to my knees and yell my prayer as loud as I could. I figured only God and the cows could hear me.

"God, please deliver me from these cursed cows!" I would scream. "I hate them!"

This went on for three months. Nobody but God and the cows knew of these angry prayers. I never told Victor or Nastia how I felt, because I knew it wouldn't help.

But then God responded in a most unusual way. One autumn day after I had herded the cows home, Nastia called me into her kitchen.

"Vanya, sit down and eat some vareniki," Nastia said. The smell and sight of this savory feast set my mouth watering with anticipation. But as I gulped down that first bite, I looked up at Nastia and saw tears forming in her eyes.

"What's the matter, Aunt Nastia? Why are you crying?"

"Vanyushka, I don't exactly know what it is, but deep inside my heart I hear a voice saying, 'What would you do if it were your own son sitting in his place?' You know I have a son your age, and I care for him very much. I would hate to see him in your situation. Vanyushka, that voice is telling me to release you from herding our cattle."

My breath was snatched right out of my lungs. I began choking, trying to hold back my tears.

O Lord, I thought. *When I screamed out my prayers in those deserted hills, it seemed like only the cows were listening. Thank you for answering.*

"I will arrange everything," Nastia said. "When my husband comes home, you tell him you don't want to herd our cattle any longer. But don't tell him I told you to say so. He will try to convince you to remain because he likes you and you're a good worker. But don't agree, or else you'll be a shepherd for the rest of your life. I want you to go to Gulja. I know Masha, my sister, will probably beat you, but afterward you'll be able to find some better work in the city. You may even be able to study and make something of yourself."

I was stunned as I stared at Nastia. God was miraculously answering my prayers through Mama's sister. No more dust, no more cursed cows. A tear slid off my cheek and landed on my plate. "Nastia, I . . . I . . . can hardly believe my ears. Thank you for caring enough for me to think about my future."

Wiping away her own tears, Nastia said, "Now make sure to finish all your food and get ready to talk to Victor. He should be home very soon."

When Victor came home, he desperately tried to convince me to stay and continue herding their cattle. But I stood firm. Every so often, I would glance over at Nastia, and she would wink at me. Try as he may, Victor could not convince me to stay.

After nearly six months of my living with Victor and Nastia— and their stinking cows—God was again moving me on, to what I did not know. Victor had asked a sheepherder on his way to Gulja to take me along as a helper. For the next twenty days, as the shepherd rode ahead in a wagon, I slowly followed behind, herding his twenty sheep. I couldn't get rid of the lice no matter how hard I tried. My clothes were filthy, and I didn't know whether I itched more from dust or from lice. The alkaline dust burned my eyes so badly that by the time we reached Gulja, I could barely see.

It didn't matter. Gulja was where my real mama was buried. And somewhere near here were Marusia, Misha, and Lena. How I longed to see them and the Shevchenkos.

We herded the sheep to a large open-air market on the outskirts of town. After we had penned them up, the shepherd took me to the house where Papa and Mama were staying. Nastia must have told him where they lived. Mama was shocked when she opened the door and saw me standing there. After thanking the shepherd, she dragged me into the house by my ear.

"What are you doing in Gulja!" Mama screamed as she twisted my ear.

"Nas . . . Nastia told me I didn't have to herd the cattle anymore and that I should come to Gulja," I explained, wincing with pain.

"What about our cows? You were supposed to look after them, you little lazy dog!" Mama slapped me, and I fell to the floor. Then she took out her strap and began thrashing me. Even though her blows hurt me, something was different with Masha. I could tell she was hurting too. "What am I going to do with you now?" she moaned.

Suddenly Mama began pacing the floor and pulling at her hair. "Ivan is dead and I'm all alone. O God! Why did You take Ivan home so soon?"

Papa is dead?

Mama slumped to the floor and began to weep. I wanted to go over and hug her, but I didn't dare. She had been so cruel that I didn't know how she would react. But I felt genuine compassion for her. I didn't think she'd let me hug her, but I still got up and walked over to her. Placing my hand on her shoulder, I started to say, "Mama, I'm sorry Pa—"

"Get your hands off me!" she yelled. "I told Ivan I didn't need you four years ago, and I don't need you now. I always wanted a little girl, not some mutt of a boy. I'm finally going to get rid of you!"

Pulling me up by my ear, Mama dragged me toward the door. As she pushed me out, I tumbled down the front step. Mama kicked me and shouted, "Get up, you little dog! I'm sick and tired of your disobedience and laziness."

Mama half pushed, half dragged me for several blocks till we arrived at a big house. I noticed all sorts of people going in and wondered where Mama had brought me. Mama suddenly got very nice, greeting people and shaking their hands. As I looked more closely at the house, I recognized it. It was our church building. This was Wednesday night, and Mama had brought me to church.

"Well, well, who do we have here?"

I spun around to see who was talking to me and looked up at Alex Shevchenko.

"Is that you, Vanya?" Alex asked, breaking out into a broad grin.

"Hello, Alex," I said, thrusting out my hand toward him.

"My, how you've grown. How old are you?"

"I'll be ten next month."

Looking at Mama, he said, "Masha, it looks like you've done a good job raising Vanya these past four years. Everyone is grateful to you and your late husband for taking Vanya. Now let's get into church or we'll be late."

Mama strode toward the front of the church. We sat on the left side with all the women. The men and older boys sat on the right. Before we walked in, Mama tied a scarf on her head. All the married women wore scarves in church. I had heard many a sermon explaining how a woman's head must be covered as a sign of submission and reverence to God. No woman could pray with her head uncovered.

Sitting next to Mama, I could see only women with colorful scarves on their heads. I felt embarrassed to be sitting on the women's side. After all, I was almost ten years old. But I sat silently.

The church choir began singing hymns, and I was thrilled to see Alex leading the choir. Next came some prayers, more hymns, and then a brief sermon by the pastor. I loved to hear the choir sing in four-part harmony and decided that as soon as I was old enough, I was going to sing in the choir, just like my papa had.

The program wasn't long. Only a few poems were read, and a solo was sung by a young girl. After the offering, one of the men in the congregation delivered a closing sermon. Then we all prayed again, only this time we got on our knees. This was usually the end of the service, except that the pastor would ask whether anyone had any greetings to pass on or had anything to say. I was getting ready to walk out when Mama stood up.

"As all of you know, my husband, Ivan, recently passed away. For the past four years we have been taking care of Vanya Yakovich, the orphan boy."

Mama pulled me up by my shoulders.

"He has been more of a burden to us than anything. With Ivan dead, I no longer have any need of him, and I don't want him. You can have him back."

The room began to buzz with conversation, but I was too embarrassed to look up. Mama—or should I call her Masha now—sat down next to me. I noticed her head was tilted backward and she had a stern look on her face. I wanted to run and hide in some dark corner where no one could see me cry. Yes, I was glad that Masha would no longer be my mama, but another part of me felt totally rejected.

I could hear two women behind me whispering, "I wonder why she no longer wants him?"

"I don't know, but look how skinny he is."

"But he's Yakov and Pelageya's boy. He can't be all that bad."

By now everyone was speaking at once, some actually shouting. The pastor finally restored order and, looking down at me, said, "You all know Yakov and Pelageya Iliyn. This is their youngest son. Since Masha no longer wants him, we need to find a new home for him. Is there anybody here who would like Vanya to live with them?"

For the longest time nobody spoke. People kept whispering back and forth. Someone finally spoke up. "We'll take Vanya."

I turned to see who had said this and saw a man walking toward the front. "We have no children and just have my mother-in-law living with us." The man looked at me and smiled.

The pastor also smiled and said, "Thank you, Vasil, for agreeing to take Vanya. Please tell your wife, Marusia, thank you for us. And may God bless you."

As the service ended, Masha stormed past me and out of the building. I never did have a chance to say goodbye. As I watched her leave, I felt relief that I would no longer have to endure her verbal attacks and beatings. But once again I was heading into an unknown future with parents who were strangers to me. My stomach was in knots.

"Vanya, my name is Vasil Kondtratiev."

I jerked my head around and found myself face-to-face with a strange, kind face. The man thrust his hand toward me, and a big smile broke out on his face. As I tentatively stretched my hand toward his, I softly mumbled, "Hello, Uncle Vasil." I couldn't call him Papa yet and decided to call him Uncle Vasil, a polite way Papa and Mama had taught me to address adults.

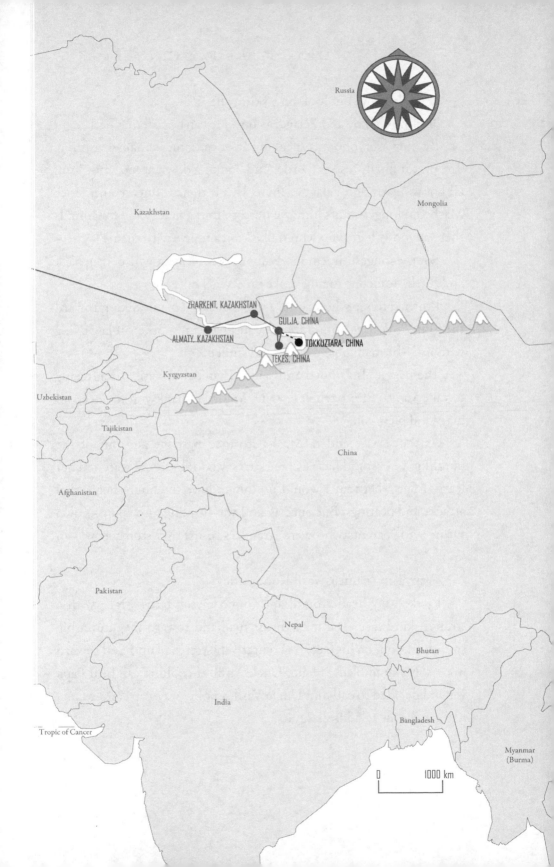

SEVEN

"WHERE'S TOKKUZTARA?" I asked Uncle Vasil. That was the name of the city where he and Aunt Marusia lived and where I would now live. Shortly after the church service ended, Uncle Vasil and I left Gulja in his wagon.

"It's about one hundred kilometers southeast of Gulja."

I looked up at Uncle Vasil's gentle eyes and realized for the first time in four years I wasn't afraid. I felt strangely secure sitting next to him in his wagon, watching him skillfully handle his big black horse. I only wished he would urge his horse to move quicker. What if Mama . . . er . . . Masha were to change her mind and come after me? A dark sense of dread crept over me as I glanced toward Gulja, half expecting to see Masha running after us, grabbing for my ears. My body tensed up, and sweat began trickling down my neck. I could almost feel Masha's hand yanking me back to Gulja.

"Faster, go faster!" I yelled.

"Vanya, what's the matter?" Uncle Vasil's eyes locked onto mine, and I saw his genuine concern for me. Only then did my fear began to disappear.

"I . . . I thought Ma . . . Ma . . . Masha was coming to take me back to Gulja," I stammered.

Uncle Vasil reached over with his strong arm and placed it on my shoulder, snuggling me up against his side.

"No one is taking you back to Gulja." His gentle yet firm voice brought a sense of security and love that I had yearned for so much over the past five years.

"Look, Vanya, the Ili River." I followed Uncle Vasil's outstretched hand and saw the quick-flowing river just ahead of us. Uncle Vasil explained that its icy cold waters came from the snowmelt on the Tien Shan, the high, white mountains to the south. As we rode up onto the old ferry and the mechanical pulley began slowly pulling us across, I sneaked one last look across the desert valley toward Gulja. No Masha! I thanked God and looked at the other shore. Somewhere beyond was my future.

Uncle Vasil and Aunt Marusia Kondtratiev lived in a small house right in the middle of Tokkuztara. Like the other towns I'd seen in western China, it was a hot, dusty place with people of various races mostly making a living from herding, farming, or trading. I liked my new home. Uncle Vasil and Aunt Marusia treated me very kindly, yet for some reason I couldn't call them Papa and Mama. Perhaps I had come to realize I had only one papa and one mama and they were in heaven.

Uncle Vasil repaired sewing machines and usually did his work in people's homes. Aunt Marusia would accompany him and help with the repairs. I was often left home alone with Babushka (Grandma) Olga, Aunt Marusia's mother. Babushka was a short, stout Russian woman with gray hair pulled into a bun. Her face was etched with wrinkles, but her brown eyes seemed young and bright. She helped me with my chores and taught me much about my new surroundings.

My chores included working in Aunt Marusia's garden and caring for their chickens and cows. The first time I saw these chickens, painful memories filled my mind. I instinctively reached for my ears, half expecting them to be bleeding. Every time I walked into the house with my hands full of eggs, my body became rigid. It took a full month before I could relax around chickens and eggs.

Babushka reminded me a lot of Mama, my real mama, that is. Every night, after a long day of work, Babushka would feed me and tuck me into bed and sing songs to me. I loved these songs and soon was singing them with her. We spent many an evening singing about Jesus and heaven. This became my favorite time of day.

One night while Uncle Vasil and Aunt Marusia were away on business and I was sound asleep, I was awakened by someone yanking at my sleeve. I popped open my eyes and there, not two inches away from my nose, was Babushka's terrified face.

"Someone's trying to break into the house!" she whispered as she grabbed my arm and pulled me out of bed. Her voice was trembling. She was pointing toward the back of the house when I heard someone beating on our door and yelling.

Babushka began pushing me from behind, and I reluctantly slid forward.

"What's he saying, Babushka?"

"Sounds like he's saying, 'You had better open this door or I'll tear it down!'"

Babushka's grip on my shoulder suddenly tightened. She leaned over to my left ear and whispered, "I think he's a *sheebeenitz*!"

Here I was, a ten-year-old boy trying to stop a sheebeenitz from breaking into our home. Sheebeentzi were notorious criminals who rarely, if ever, showed any mercy to their victims.

"Vanya, say to him in his Musulmanski language, 'May God curse you!'" Babushka's voice didn't sound all that convincing.

Misha had taught me some Musulmanski words, but I couldn't remember how to say *curse* in their language. By now, we were standing near the back door. I could make out the Mongol features of the man outside and actually saw his fat fingers beginning to pry open our door. The latch was coming loose. Soon it would be too late.

"Vanya, say something!" Babushka screamed. The sheebeenitz was bellowing louder and louder, and the door was on the verge of crumbling.

Closing my eyes, I screamed as loud as I could, "May God kill you!"

I thought for sure those murderous fingers would soon be wrapped around my neck.

My eyes were tightly shut. I prayed. I waited. Suddenly all noise ceased. All I could hear was Babushka's heavy breathing and someone running away. I opened my eyes and glanced at the door.

"What happened?" I asked.

Babushka released her grip on my shoulder. "As soon as you shouted at him, he froze in his tracks, then turned and ran away."

Babushka's body suddenly went limp. I looked up at her face and saw her wrinkles melt into the most beautiful smile I had ever seen. We began to laugh, and together we slid down to the floor. We sat on the floor a long time, laughing and thanking God for protecting us.

Babushka became my closest friend. We often worked together, like the time a few months later when Uncle Vasil told me to hitch up the wagon and go collect roots in the countryside. Uncle would dry the roots and use them as fuel for our woodstove.

The wagon had no seat, and so Babushka and I sat inside it on cushions she had brought along. Babushka had also brought a lunch basket full of bread and homemade sausages. Uncle Vasil's big black horse had no problem pulling us along. By the time we found the root field, it was almost noon. We ate our lunch and then set out to work.

I would dig the roots and pile them next to the wagon. Babushka would bundle them and load them into the wagon. Once the roots were piled as high as we could stack them, we would crawl up on top of them and head home. That's what Uncle Vasil told us to do.

After several hours of digging, I noticed that the wagon was getting rather full. But I continued gathering roots, assuming Babushka would tell me when to stop. I was pulling more out of the dry ground when I heard a loud thump and an ear-piercing scream.

I dropped my shovel and ran toward the wagon. As I rounded the wagon, there was Babushka, slumped on the ground, leaning awkwardly against the wagon. Her face was riddled with pain. I knelt beside her and said, "What happened, Babushka?"

It was then that I noticed how tenderly she was holding her right hand. Her wrist was twisted, and a bone was almost protruding through her skin.

"I . . . I was trying to climb up onto the wagon and slipped and fell on my right hand." Babushka was in so much pain she could barely speak. "My wrist is . . . is broken. Vanyushka, you're going to have to twist it back."

I was horrified. I wanted to say no, but who else could help us? As I touched her wrist, Babushka screamed. I dropped her wrist and wanted to run away.

"Go ahead, Vanyushka. Please don't mind my screaming." Babushka was crying now as she spoke. Once again I reached out and took her wrist into my hands. As I began twisting it back, Babushka grabbed my shoulder with her left hand and squeezed. She began pounding her legs against the ground as I twisted her wrist. I could hear her bones clicking and saw the protruding bone disappear. Babushka was moaning deeply.

When I finally got her wrist straight, I felt an intense pain in my right shoulder.

"Babushka, please let go of my shoulder!" I screamed.

She opened her eyes, let go of my shoulder, and looked approvingly at her now-straightened right wrist.

"Oh, Vanyushka. What are we going to do?"

I knew I would have to get Babushka on top of the roots, but how?

"My wrist, it hurts so bad, Vanyushka." Babushka looked like she might faint.

I grabbed her left hand and began pulling her up. As Babushka struggled to her feet, I noticed a rope near the back wheel of the wagon.

"Babushka, I have an idea." I rushed over and picked up the rope.

"Here, Babushka. Let's tie this rope around your waist."

She was too weak to protest. I quickly secured the rope around her waist and threw the other end over the roots to the other side of the wagon.

"Babushka, as I pull the rope, you're going to have to use your good hand and crawl up onto the roots."

Even as I spoke, I could see the impossibility of the situation. Babushka was far too heavy for me to hoist up onto the wagon, and her right wrist was useless.

As I ran around to the other side of the wagon, I prayed, "Father,

I really need Your help. Please give Babushka the strength to pull herself onto the roots and get us home safely."

"Babushka, I'm going to start pulling the rope," I told her. "Start climbing onto the wagon."

Babushka's scream of pain caused me to stop pulling. Then I heard her yell, "Pull, Vanyushka, pull!"

I pulled as hard as I could in spite of Babushka's painful yelps. When I thought my chest would burst and my legs collapse, I heard her say, "Vanyushka, stop pulling. I made it."

As I let go of the rope, I lost my balance and toppled to the ground. But as I looked up, there was Babushka, lying on top of the roots. I was elated and exhausted. I still don't know how Babushka got up on those roots. I think an angel pushed her up.

After collecting our tools, I crawled up next to Babushka, who just lay there cradling her right wrist on her chest and moaning. I knew I needed to get her home as soon as I could. I grabbed the reins, and the wagon jerked forward. Babushka screamed. As the roots shifted and settled, she had started sliding off. I twisted to the right, grabbed her left arm, and yanked on the reins. Babushka screamed again.

I had to do something quickly. I grabbed the rope lying next to Babushka. I took one end and tied it around my belt. Not knowing what else to do, I wound the rope several times around Babushka's neck and shoulders. That seemed to hold her down, but each bump in the road caused her obvious pain.

I was desperate to get Babushka home safely, and the horse quickened his pace as the sun began sliding behind the mountains. The last part of our return was in full darkness, but our horse knew the road home. Babushka moaned and cried all the way to our village. To my new family I was a hero, bringing both Babushka and the wagonload of roots home safely.

This accident and the attempted robbery incident forever cemented my relationship with Babushka, who became like a mother to me. I found myself drawn less and less toward dark corners, although I still had my special place where I could be alone to talk to my Father in heaven. No matter what the situation, Babushka always made me feel special. She spent time with me during the day and especially before bedtime. Singing songs with Babushka as we sat next to the woodstove was my favorite time of the day. Because of Babushka, I felt like I was finally part of a family.

MY FIRST YEAR with the Kondtratievs went by quickly. One of my greatest joys of that year was going fishing with Uncle Vasil. In June of 1939 Uncle Vasil surprised me by announcing that I would be joining him and his friend Peter Chikunov on a one-week fishing and hunting trip. I had never before been on such a great adventure. Early one morning, the three of us set off in our wagon. As we made our way up into the mountains, Uncle Vasil pointed out all the good fishing spots. We passed several lakes before finally stopping to fish.

Uncle Vasil looked a bit confused as he surveyed the lake. Apparently we had gone too far up the mountain and had missed the best fishing spot. Uncle Vasil suggested that Peter and I take the boat and provisions and make our way to the fishing spot while he drove the wagon to that area. As Uncle Vasil trotted away, Peter and I began rowing in the direction he had shown us. The lake was calm and crowded with other boats, and I was relaxed, knowing Peter had fished with Uncle Vasil and knew where we were to meet up.

After an hour of rowing, Peter stood up in the boat and started looking around. I heard him gasp and rush back to his seat.

"What's the matter?" I said.

"Something is wrong. This isn't the lake anymore. We're on the Kunges River."

As he spoke, I noticed our boat was moving though we weren't rowing. The current wasn't fast, but it was pulling our boat downstream. Somehow we had entered the lake at the wrong place and were now below our intended destination. Unless Uncle Vasil realized this, he would be waiting for us at the wrong spot. We were quite far from shore and the current was moving faster. I looked straight ahead and noticed the river widening. Then I heard a distinct thundering noise.

"What's that sound I hear? Sounds just like a waterfall."

"It's the Tekes River joining up with the Kunges River," Peter said. I noticed the concern in his eyes as he picked up his oars.

"Why is it so loud?"

"The Tekes runs down from the Tien Shan, and by the time it meets up with the Kunges, it's a very fast-moving and violent river. It slams into the Kunges. That's the noise you hear and the source of all that mist. Now Vanya, grab your oars. We need to row as far away from the Tekes as we can. Hurry or we'll get sucked into it!"

The once-peaceful Kunges soon grew faster and more turbulent. Its waters were now lapping over the sides of our boat. I began furiously rowing away from "the intersection," as Peter called it. I could barely hear his shouting above the roar of the two rivers clashing. The water began swirling, pulling us toward the middle. I knew if we got sucked into the center of the funnel, we were doomed. Our only chance was to get as far away from it as possible.

The river was wide at this point, and Peter kept directing our boat toward the other side. My arms and shoulders were aching, but I knew I couldn't stop. The water was a swirling mass of waves crashing against our boat, trying to force us toward the center. Several times we almost capsized. Right when I thought I couldn't go on, our boat was suddenly flung like a rock from a slingshot around the funnel and out onto the Ili, the river formed by the joining of the Tekes and the Kunges. Peter and I were both startled. One moment we thought we were doomed, and the next moment we had hurled past the funnel, safe at last.

After bailing the water out of our boat, Peter and I began rowing toward shore. I was never happier to step onto dry land as I was then! Peter started a fire as I emptied the boat of our provisions. Both of us needed to get dry or we'd catch a chill from the crisp mountain air. As we sat next to the fire and ate, Peter told me he was going for help and that I would have to protect the boat and provisions till he got back.

As I watched him leave, I became afraid. I was all alone in a strange place. What would I do if someone tried to rob me? If someone knew I was the only one guarding all these provisions, they might even kill me. As my mind swirled with thoughts of all kinds of dangers, I heard footsteps and loud voices. I could tell it was a group of Kirghiz men, probably hunters. I knew they wouldn't think twice about robbing me. *Dear God, what should I do?*

"Hey boy, you got any matches?" they shouted.

They stood a fair distance away, and it was getting dark. I hoped they hadn't seen all our provisions.

"Sorry, I don't have any," I replied.

Suddenly, for no apparent reason, they turned around and left. They must have thought that another person, an adult, was somewhere nearby. All I could do was thank God for His protection.

After gathering branches and tall grass, I quickly made a grass hut and fell into a deep sleep. My fear had disappeared. I woke up to the voice of Peter, who had returned with a wagon and a horse. After loading all our provisions, we set off for the camp Uncle Vasil had set up. Uncle was relieved to see me alive and well. Throughout the remainder of our fishing trip, we told stories of past dangers and adventures, and each story ended the same, with thankfulness for God's protection.

Toward the end of summer in 1939, Aunt Marusia sent me on another new adventure. One day she called me into her kitchen, and there on the table were some of the biggest, plumpest green peppers I had ever seen. The peppers had come from her garden, and I knew that Aunt Marusia had spent lots of energy growing them.

"Vanya, I want you to take these peppers into town and sell them."

I had never been entrusted with a mission like this before. My mind flooded with questions. But before I could even ask them, Aunt Marusia was giving me clear instructions.

"Take them in this sack and go to the corner of our main street. Take the peppers out of the sack and spread them out on top of the sack. Sell them for one *jiao* each, and here's three jiao for your lunch. You have fifty peppers, so you should come home with about fifty jiao."

The sack was large, but I flung it over my shoulder and set out to town. It was Saturday, and I noticed more people on the streets than usual. I found my corner, carefully spread the peppers out on the sack, and squatted, ready to sell them.

I was proud of Aunt Marusia's green peppers. They looked bigger and greener than all the others being sold all around me. As I was looking at other vendors, I heard someone say, "Hey, little boy. How much for your green peppers?"

I jerked my head around and was face-to-face with a short, stocky Musulman. His mustache was almost wider than his face.

"Uh, they're one jiao apiece, sir."

"You got some nice-looking peppers. Give me three," he said.

As I took his money, I noticed more people eyeing our peppers.

"Hey, boy. I want two peppers."

I followed the voice and saw two babushkas and one younger fellow squatting to my right. Each was picking up peppers and twisting them around.

"These peppers are better than any I have seen all day," I overheard one of the babushkas say.

Now more people were crowding around the peppers. Everyone was talking at once. As I was taking money and giving change, I noticed people grabbing my peppers and running off.

"They're stealing my peppers!"

But before I could do anything, someone else was giving me money and waiting for change. By the time the crowd thinned out, I had one third of the peppers left. Quickly counting my money, I realized about one fourth of my peppers had been stolen.

I felt sick. It was almost lunchtime, and even though I was famished, I tossed my lunch money into the money bag. Then I tried selling my peppers for more money, but very few people bought them. After finally selling the remaining peppers, I set off for home.

My stomach was growling, and my heart was racing.

"What will I say to Aunt Marusia when she counts the money?"

Dread crept over me as I approached our house. I could see Aunt Marusia through the window. I tried making it around to the back without her seeing me, when suddenly our eyes met. I froze in my tracks. Aunt Marusia motioned for me to come into the house.

"Back so soon, Vanya?" Aunt Marusia was wiping her hands on her apron as I walked into the kitchen. "I see you sold all my peppers. Where's the money bag?" she asked. As I handed the bag to her, I tried saying something, but no sound came out of my mouth.

Aunt Marusia counted the money a lot faster than I could have. She stiffened.

"Vanya, some of the money is missing. Where is it?"

Her eyes bore down on me, and her face seemed to change. It was as if I was looking into the eyes of Masha. Suddenly I wanted to run and hide in some dark corner. I wanted to be alone, in a place where no one would misunderstand me.

"Vanya!" She startled me with her shout.

"I . . . I . . . don't know where the money went. I sold all the—"

"You're lying to me, aren't you?" Aunt Marusia started taking her apron off.

I stood frozen in my tracks.

"After all I've done for you, and still you try to steal from me." She started walking toward me.

"Aunt Marusia, I never stole anything from you."

"Get out!" Aunt Marusia lunged at me, grabbed my shoulder twisting me toward the door, and began pushing me.

"Please, Auntie, listen to me!" I pleaded with her. "I didn't steal the money. I saw several people steal peppers, but I couldn't do anything about it. I even put my lunch money into the bag and haven't eaten all day. Please believe me!"

Aunt Marusia flung the door open and, pushing me out, screamed, "Get out and don't come back!"

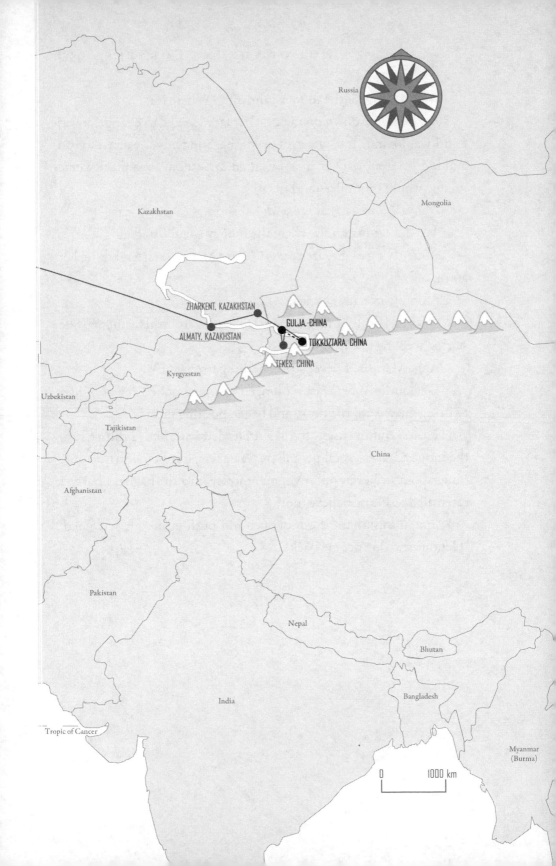

EIGHT

AS I TRIPPED and went sprawling on the ground, I heard the door shut behind me. I could still hear Aunt Marusia's last words, "And don't come back!"

I sat up too stunned to even react. And then it hit me. "No, God! Not again!"

Through my tears, I looked back at my home and began sobbing uncontrollably. That horrible feeling of loneliness cut me like a knife to the heart.

At least I have Misha and my sisters, I thought. *But they live so far away. O God, what do I do?*

I wanted to run, to find my own place, alone, where I could talk to my Father. I saw Aunt Marusia's garden, and suddenly my feet were carrying me into the garden. As I ran, I wept and flailed my arms. My mind was racing. I could barely make out a grove of trees

Thailand

Philippines

ahead of me. I dived face-first onto the grass and cried and cried and cried.

"God, it wasn't my fault those peppers were stolen. Why didn't she believe me?"

From deep within my soul I groaned, "Why, God, did You take Papa and Mama from me? Take me home. I don't want to live anymore. Take me home."

I cried a very long time under those trees.

"Oh, Vanyushka." I was startled by the gentle, familiar voice of Babushka. Looking up at her blurred face, I wiped away my tears and gladly melted into her outstretched arms.

"My dear Vanyushka. Don't cry. Marusia didn't mean what she said. Don't worry. I'll talk to her and convince her to take you back."

Babushka's consoling words brought a ray of hope back into my spirit.

"Babushka, I . . . I didn't steal the money." Tears began flooding down my cheeks again. "Some people at the marketplace. . . . They . . . they stole them . . ."

"Now, now, Vanyushka. I understand."

I could see my tear stains running down Babushka's dress as she held me tight. Babushka began singing one of our favorite songs as she gently rocked me. I finally stopped sobbing.

"Get up, Vanyushka. Let's go and talk to Marusia."

My fear was gone as together we walked into the house. Somehow I knew that Aunt Marusia would understand that it wasn't my fault and would take me back.

"Marusia," Babushka began, "take Vanyushka back. You misunderstood what happened. It wasn't his fault, and he wasn't lying to you. Listen to his story one more time."

Aunt Marusia didn't look too convinced, but she grudgingly permitted me to tell my side of the story. When I finally finished, Aunt Marusia looked down at me. "Alright. You can come back, but let this be the last time something like this happens."

I turned and hugged Babushka. I felt her warmth as she embraced me.

Turning and looking up at Aunt Marusia, I said, "Thank you, Aunt Marusia, for letting me stay." Although her hug was rather stiff, it didn't bother me. I was just glad to have a home.

And it really became my home.

Uncle Vasil started taking me with him on his work trips. We traveled to many different villages, fixing sewing machines everywhere we went. Uncle Vasil even started teaching me how to fix them.

When I grow up, I began thinking, *I want to be just like Uncle Vasil.*

The painful memories of my life with Masha almost didn't seem real. I even soon forgot about my green pepper affair with Aunt Marusia. I finally felt loved and cared for. I felt I was home.

IN SEPTEMBER OF 1940 everything changed. Uncle Vasil and Aunt Marusia had gone to Gulja for work reasons. When they returned, Uncle Vasil called me into the kitchen.

"Vanya, come sit at the table. I have some news for you from your brother."

"Misha! You saw Misha? How is he? What did he say? Did he—"

Uncle Vasil chuckled. "Now, now, Vanya. Just sit down!"

I jumped onto the stool and could hardly wait for Uncle Vasil to speak.

"Aunt Marusia and I spent some time with Mitrofan and Maria, your real uncle and aunt. They had just returned from Aksu and were planning to go back soon. Misha, your brother, was with them, and he asked us to give you this message. They want you to go with them to Aksu."

"To Aksu!" I shouted as I leapt off the stool.

But then I slowly sat down and, looking at Uncle and Aunt, said, "You mean they want me to leave you, Babushka, and my home?"

"Yes, Vanya. Misha wants you to go live with them in Aksu. Marusia, your older sister, is also going."

Somewhere deep in my heart I wanted to be with my brother and sister, but this was home. For a split second I struggled with my decision, but then I cried out, "I can't leave you. You're my family now. No, I will not go. I want to live with you and Babushka."

"Vanya," Aunt Marusia said. "We're so glad you feel that way. We love you and want you to be our son."

I wasn't sure what she meant by that, but then Uncle cleared it up.

"Yes, Vanya. If you feel that way, we would like to adopt you as our legal son."

I felt my chest heave up into my throat as I looked over at a beaming smile from Babushka.

"What do you think of that, Vanyushka?" Babushka said.

I couldn't remain silent anymore and burst out in laughter mixed with tears.

"Thank you, thank you, thank you!" was all that came out of my mouth as I hugged everyone. After hugging Uncle, I looked up and said, "Does this mean I can call you Papa and Mama?"

Uncle Vasil had tears in his eyes as he grabbed me by the shoulders and said loudly, "Yes, son, we are your papa and mama."

I was overwhelmed with joy, and once again I hugged Babushka and my new papa and mama.

"Vanya, tomorrow we're going back to Gulja, and you need to come with us."

"To Gulja?" I said. "I'll be able to see Misha and Marusia and tell them this good news!"

Papa continued, "Vanya, Misha and Mitrofan asked us to bring you back to Gulja so that you could go with them to Aksu. But now that you want to stay with us, you need to personally tell them of your decision."

"Then that's what I will do," I said confidently.

Papa said we would be leaving early the next morning. Babushka was up before dawn to say goodbye. I gave her a hug and promised to bring her something from Gulja. As the wagon pulled away, I looked back and smiled at the sight of Babushka and my first true home.

The two-hundred-kilometer trip to Gulja took two weeks. On the way we passed many villages, and it seemed like Papa had a special story about each one. He knew which homes had sewing machines, most of which had been serviced by his master's touch. Papa promised to teach me all he knew and to take me with him now that I was going to be his son. I felt wanted, secure, and happy.

As we approached Gulja, the noise and clutter shocked me. I had forgotten how big Gulja was. People were everywhere. The streets

were lined with vendors selling their wares from small open stalls. As
we approached a shoe stall, Papa reined the horse to an abrupt halt.

"Vanya, come with us. We want to buy you something," he said.

Papa and Mama took me to the shoe stall and picked out a brand
new pair of leather sandals.

"Vanya, in celebration of your becoming our son, we want you to
have these sandals. Try them on, son."

I felt proud and happy as I slipped on my first new pair of sandals. They fit just right, and I was sure everyone was looking at me as
I took a few steps. Papa didn't want me to wear them just yet, and I
reluctantly took them off. As I hugged Papa and Mama, I felt more
and more like their son.

From there, they took me directly to the Shevchenkos' home,
where Uncle Mitrofan and my brother Misha were staying. As we
pulled up to their house, my mind flooded with memories. I remembered how Alex had carried me through the rice fields when Mama
was lost and Papa was too weak to hold me. I remembered living with
them right after Mama died. Coming here was like coming home for
me. As I jumped down from the wagon, I heard someone shouting
my name.

"Vanya! Vanya! Is that really you?"

I knew that voice. As I turned to see where it was coming from, I
caught a glimpse of someone running toward me.

"Misha!" I yelled.

All I could see was a blur as Misha flew through the air and
pounced on me. Together we rolled on the ground, laughing and
hugging each other.

"Vanya, it's so good to see you!" Misha's curly brown hair was a
mess after our romp on the ground.

"I think the last time I saw you was when you came to Gulja with Uncle Vasil about six months ago. Is he still teaching you how to fix sewing machines?" he asked.

"Yes, Misha. Not only is he teaching me how to fix sewing machines; he told me that one of these days I would take over his business."

I noticed that Misha didn't share my excitement. Still, I had to share my most exciting news with him.

"Misha, I no longer call them Uncle and Aunt, they are my Papa and Mama. I finally have a real home and a family. I'm going to be adopted!"

Misha's reaction caught me off guard. His normally bright, happy eyes looked sad and his shoulders drooped.

"Papa bought me a new pair of leather sandals as a special gift for his new son!"

I was beaming from ear to ear, expecting Misha to congratulate me. Instead, he stood up, grabbed me by my shoulders and said, "Come home with me. I need to talk to you."

I told Mama I'd be staying with Misha and followed him to the Shevchenkos' home, where he and Marusia, my oldest sister, were staying. Misha seemed glad that nobody was home when we arrived. He took me to his room and sat me on his bed. I knew from his serious look that he had something important to tell me.

"Vanya, Marusia and I are leaving with Uncle Mitrofan to Aksu. We want you to come with us."

"I can't go. I finally have a real home with a papa and a mama. They promised to adopt me and for the first time make me part of a real family. I love them, Misha."

My brother squatted on the floor in front of me and stared straight into my eyes. "Vanya, listen to me. Uncle Vasil and Aunt Marusia can't replace us, your real family. Remember the time you were kicked out of their house? You told me about it the last time you visited Gulja."

"But Misha, that was just a misunderstanding. They're my family now, and that won't happen again," I said, trying to sound sure of myself.

Misha grabbed my hands. "But suppose it does, Vanya. Then what? Where will you go? Marusia and I will be too far away to help you. What will you do?"

No, I thought, *it won't happen, it couldn't happen again. Or could it?*

Doubt began to creep into my mind. It had happened once, and it might happen again. I suddenly remembered how I felt, sobbing under the grove of trees with nowhere to go, no one to care for me. How I wanted to die, to go to heaven. My only string of hope was knowing that Misha and Marusia were in Gulja. But now they were leaving. I had never before felt this torn in my life. Should I leave my papa and mama and go with my brother and sister? *O God, what should I do?*

"Vanya, you have to come with us. We're your true family."

As Misha said these words, suddenly it became clear to me. I had to go with them. I couldn't risk being rejected again, being kicked out and left alone. I needed to be with my brother and sister.

"Okay, I'll go!"

Misha grabbed my face and kissed my cheek.

"You won't regret your decision, Vanya. That I can promise you."

My mind agreed, but my heart hurt. What will Papa and Mama say?

"I have got to tell the Kondtratievs my decision," I said as I got up to go.

Misha bounced up besides me. "I'll go with you."

"No," I replied. "I think I'd better speak to them alone."

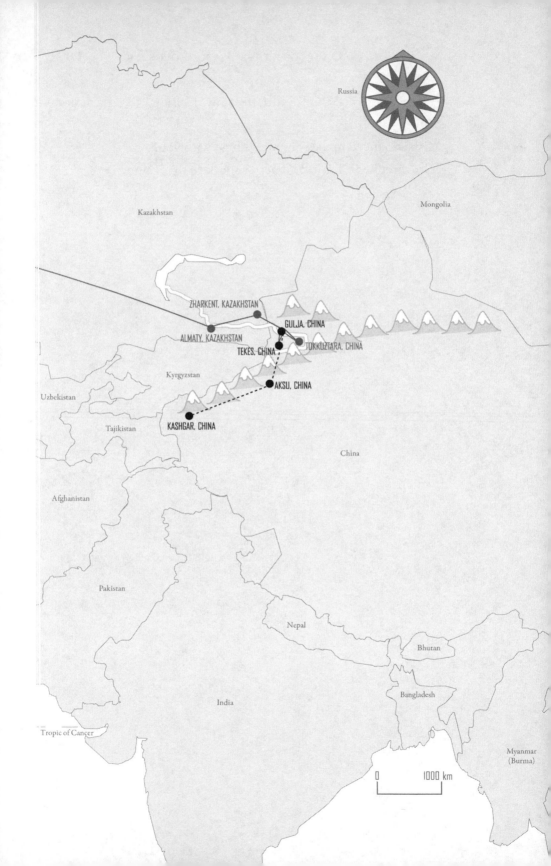

NINE

CAN'T BELIEVE THIS!" It was the first time I had heard Papa raise his voice at me. Papa stood up and began pacing frantically.

"But why, Vanya?" he continued. "I thought you agreed to become our son. We were planning to adopt you."

"How could you do this to us?" Mama added. "After all we did for you, this is how you repay us? How dare you!"

Something in Mama's voice made me recall the day she kicked me out of the house. Her eyes frightened me.

"I'm truly sorry for hurting you," I said, "but my decision is final. I want to be with my brother and sister."

I could see both sadness and anger in Papa's eyes as he said, "Fine, Vanya. If that's your decision, so be it. Go, join your family. We're leaving right now to go back to Tokkuztara."

As he turned away, I spied my new sandals. Papa must have seen them about the same time, because he picked them up, turned to me,

Thailand

Philippines

and said, "Since I don't have a son anymore, I don't have anyone to give these sandals to."

As I watched them leave Gulja in their wagon, I ached at the thought of never seeing them or Babushka again. *Dear God, did I make the right decision?*

I didn't have long to think about my decision, because within two weeks we were on our way to Aksu. It was now October 1940.

Misha bought two horses and a mule. The eleven-day trip to Aksu apparently was quite arduous, but the road was well traveled by merchants and traders. Mules were essential to carry one's belongings, as was a horse for those who couldn't walk very far. Our small group included Misha, Marusia, and me, plus Uncle Mitrofan and two other men. Aunt Maria and Dedushka were already in Aksu waiting for us.

The trip to Tekes didn't take long, but from there the path led straight up to the *muzdavan,* the Kirghiz word for a glacier. The Tien Shan mountain range loomed on both sides of the glacier, with Khan Tengri Mountain rising up seven thousand meters. Breathtaking was not quite strong enough to describe these mountains—they were the highest peaks I had ever seen.

The well-worn path up to the glacier was crowded with colorful Kirghiz and Kazakh merchants and their pack mules straining under loads of dried fruit and spices. The trek up this side of the mountain was uneventful, just plain tiring. Being the youngest, I got to ride the horse quite a bit, along with Marusia. In the years we'd been apart, she had blossomed into full womanhood, and she seemed far more serious and mature now. I sensed she also had suffered as an orphan, but she was reluctant to talk about it.

Marusia's left hand, which I recalled being bent so awkwardly, was now about half the size of her right hand. Misha told me that five years earlier, a doctor in Gulja cut out the broken bone that had never

healed, thus reducing Marusia's hand to half its normal size. But at
least the constant pain and oozing pus were gone. I asked Marusia if
she knew anything of our sister Lena, and she said that Lena was living
with a family and going to school in a city called Urümqi, far to the
northeast. It had been almost five years since we had parted, and as we
plodded along, I wondered whether I would ever see Lena again.

Walking up the glacier was not too difficult, though the ice was
cold and slippery. We tried to stick to the well-worn trails cut into
the glacier by previous trekkers. Often we would be forced to cut
new steps where the old ones had crumbled. I especially enjoyed the
meter-wide cracks we had to cross. Misha and I would always throw
rocks into the cracks and listen for the eventual splash in the stream
below. Many times we couldn't even hear it. Getting the mules over
the cracks was not so easy. We were grateful that the merchants had
built narrow walkways over the cracks for mules and horses to cross.

From the top of the glacier we could see a green valley below.
We had climbed a good four thousand meters, and the zigzagging ice
steps on this side didn't appear too safe. Uncle Mitrofan led our two
horses and pack mule step by step. The stairs were so narrow in places
that it was impossible for two people, much less two animals, to pass.
Several times my horse slipped, falling to its knees. Misha once lost
his balance and careened down the stairs till he was stopped by an ice
wall. Fortunately, he wasn't hurt.

We constantly carved new steps into the glacier. The old ones
either cracked or melted as we made our way down the ice. The glacier spawned a fast-moving river, and we had to cross its freezing
waters several times on our way down the mountain. We could tell
that the valley below us was warm but were not prepared for the stark
difference in temperature. As we took the final step off the glacier, we
were met with a blast of desert heat almost as if a furnace had been
turned on.

We took shelter that night at a *caravanserai* that was carved right out of the side of a mountain. The inn had no separate rooms, just dusty carpets on which to sleep. As I found a spot to lie down, my senses were bombarded by the smell of freshly baked bread. All around us, weary travelers—many of them Kazakh and Kirghiz traders—were slumped on the ground. Some were sleeping, but most were eating and chattering in their native languages. When I saw the *tookachi* (flat bread) they were eating, my mouth began to water.

Uncle Mitrofan saw me gazing at the bread and bought some to share. I ripped mine in half, stuffed it in my mouth, and then closed my eyes. The taste of the still-warm bread transported me back to that time on the border when I first held and smelled this flat bread. Papa was just lifting his head from prayer when everything became a blur. Horses, policemen, screaming, dust flying everywhere. My bread—I wanted to eat it, but it was gone. And Papa—I reached out to him, but he also was gone. My family. How I wanted to be part of a family. But Mama was also gone. Maybe I should have stayed with Uncle Vasil and Aunt Marusia. Had I made a mistake? Would I ever be part of a real family again?

"Vanya! Why aren't you eating?"

I looked up to see Misha with a puzzled look on his face.

"I . . . I was just remembering something."

The tookach was still in my hands, and my mouth was still stuffed. I slowly ate the bread but couldn't shake my thoughts.

As we lay down to sleep, I leaned into Misha. "What's it been like for you since Papa and Mama died? Have you ever felt like you were part of a family?"

"Why are you asking, Vanya?"

As I looked into Misha's eyes, I knew he was someone I could trust with my deepest feelings.

"The closest I've come to being part of a family was with Uncle Vasil and Aunt Marusia. I know Aunt Marusia almost kicked me out of their home, but she changed and they said they wanted to adopt me. They even bought me a new pair of sandals to celebrate my becoming their son. I really want a papa and mama, and I'm wondering now if I made the right decision."

Misha smiled. "Let me tell you what happened to me. After bouncing from home to home, I finally ended up again with the Shevchenkos. About three years ago, I became very ill and had to spend several days in the hospital. Apparently the Russian military representative in Gulja spotted me during a visit to the hospital. After inquiring about my parents, he and his wife decided to adopt me."

"Really!" I exclaimed.

I leaned closer to Misha. "So did they become family to you?"

Misha just chuckled as he continued his story.

"They sure tried making me part of their family. For the first time in my life, Vanya, I had everything I could never before have even imagined. Their house was huge. Just to get in through the gate, I had to get by several guards. And the rooms! I had never seen a house so big in my entire life. I'm sure that's why they had all those servants and maids, to clean all those rooms. The food I ate was a far cry from the bread you and I begged for on the streets of Gulja. Do you still remember?"

"How can I forget! Living like wild, hungry dogs and enduring the cold stares of people just to get a few pieces of bread to feed Mama and us."

"And I still remember the bread with all that green mold. We would just flick it off and be thankful for another piece of bread to eat."

"But what was his name?" I asked as I leaned on my elbow staring into Misha's eyes.

"His name was Oogleen."

My voice cracked and was barely audible as I asked, "Did you ever call him Papa?"

"No, Vanya. I could never call him Papa."

Misha's eyes suddenly turned sad, and he looked away.

"Was it because he beat you, like Masha beat me? Or did they kick you out of the house, like Aunt Marusia did to me?" My questions came so quickly that they surprised me.

"No, it was nothing like that, Vanya. I just couldn't walk away from everything Papa and Mama had taught us when they were alive."

Misha's eyes sparkled as he spoke, and I sat up, not wanting to miss a word.

"Oogleen tried convincing me that believing in God was foolish, just something old babushkas did. From the first day I stepped foot into his house, he did all he could to turn me into an atheist. Many evenings we sat next to the fire on huge rocking chairs talking about God. Oogleen kept repeating this phrase: religion is the opiate of the masses. He told me the people needed something to believe in, and so many had invented religion and God. Intelligent people educated in universities didn't believe in God, because they didn't need that crutch. They could solve all the world's problems with their intellect. At least that's what Oogleen wanted me to believe. According to him, man evolved from a microbe, eventually became a monkey, and then somehow turned into a man."

"What!" I exclaimed. "That's the funniest thing I have ever heard."

My brother and I started laughing so hard, our stomachs began aching.

As our laughter subsided, Misha grinned. "I wonder where the microbe came from. That's what I said to Oogleen when he told me

Misha and Marusia in Gulja, China, 1934

Church picture taken in the village of Adamovka, Ukraine, right before Yakov and Pelageya began their journey to China in spring 1927. Clockwise from top left: Mitrofan, Yakov, Marusia, and Pelageya.

Yakov

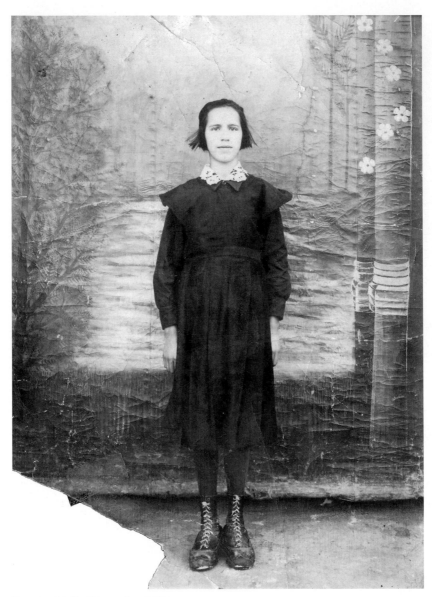

Lena in Gulja, November 1937

Gulja, spring 1938. From left: Misha, Marusia, and Vanya.

Kashgar, China, fall 1940. Back row: Marusia, Misha, and Vanya. Front row: Maria, Mitrofan, and Dedushka.

Undated photo of Dooshaijka Demchenko, the neighbor who gave Vanya eggs to protect him from Masha's beatings. Her full name is Yevdokia Gregorevna Demchenko.

Joseph and Marusia Lokteff, April 4, 1942

Misha and Nadya, April 25, 1942

this funny thing. He just smiled and couldn't answer me. For two years he tried convincing me that God didn't exist, and I kept on believing that God does exist.

"I came home one day to find two new suits lying on my bed. Next to the bed was a new suitcase, a new pair of shoes, and a briefcase. I was happy to receive these gifts but wondered why all of this was given to me now. A few days later, one of my friends told me that Oogleen had purchased for him the same gifts and was sending him, along with several other young men, to Moscow to study in a university for five years. He told me I was going too. I was shocked! Oogleen was secretly trying to send me to Russia to educate me in atheism. I decided there and then to run away and hide."

"Where did you go?" I inquired.

"I hid at Karnienko's home. Karnienko was an old man who knew me well. I didn't even tell the Shevchenkos about my plans. I knew Oogleen would send his men searching for me at their place, and sure enough, he did. I later found out that his men had gone to the Shevchenko's home several times looking for me, asking if they had heard from me."

I could barely contain my curiosity. "Did they ever find you?" I asked.

Misha's eyes lit up, and a big smile came across his face. "Nope, they never did find me. I stayed at Karnienko's home for about four days, hoping that was enough time to miss the trip to Moscow. And it was. When I finally came out of hiding, I visited the Shevchenkos, who told me that Oogleen's men were looking for me. After explaining why I had run away, I made my way home, where Oogleen confronted me."

"I bet he was mad at you," I said.

"And how!" Misha shook his head as he continued. "I can't recall ever seeing Oogleen so angry as when he interrogated me about my disappearance. He kept telling me how sorry I would be that I didn't go to Russia. I told him I would never willingly go, because I loved God and wouldn't give up my faith, even if it meant going hungry again.

"I think at that point Oogleen finally gave up trying to change me. He sent me to a local school for one year, then decided he no longer wanted to adopt me. Then another family took me in for a year. When Uncle Mitrofan arrived from Aksu, I moved in with him."

"So was that the last you saw of Oogleen?"

"No! That's the best part of the story," Misha said. "Several months ago, before you arrived at Gulja, Uncle Mitrofan and several other men were trying to secure permission to travel back to Aksu, but the military governor would not give them travel documents. The men visited the governor's office almost every day for over three months, to no avail.

"During dinner one evening, I overheard the men saying that the name of the governor's official was Oogleen. You can imagine how excited I got! I told them I had lived with Oogleen for two years and that I would be willing to go to his home and request his help. You should have heard the men laugh at me."

"Didn't they know that Oogleen almost adopted you as his son?"

Misha shook his head. "I think our older men never take us young people seriously."

"What happened next? Did you go to Oogleen? How did he treat you?"

"Hang on, little brother. Give me a chance to finish." Misha placed his hand on my shoulder and laughed.

"Yes, I went back to my, uh, his house. The guards at the gate were new and almost didn't let me in. Only after Oogleen gave the order did they finally open the gate. Oogleen and his wife were surprised to see me. They both hugged and kissed me, asking how their long lost son was doing. After I assured them I was fine, Oogleen asked what I had come for. I told him that one of the men requesting permission to travel to Aksu was my uncle. Oogleen was surprised to hear that. I then came out with my request. Would he please give us permission to travel to Aksu?

"Oogleen asked why we wanted to go to Aksu. He warned me that if it was because we wanted to escape through India, it would not work and we would be sent back to Gulja.

"After trying to dissuade me, he finally said yes, he would help us only because he still liked me and considered me almost a son. He told me to tell the men to come to his office the next morning and his staff would have the documents ready.

"Right before I left, Oogleen poured two glasses of cognac and gave me a glass. 'Now that you're almost a man,' he said, 'we need to have a drink together.' I politely declined his offer and was glad his wife interceded for me, taking the glass away."

"What happened when you told the others about this?" I asked.

"They didn't believe me and actually laughed again. But the next day, when they visited Oogleen's office, they finally received their travel documents. They didn't laugh at me after that," Misha said with a smirk.

"And so, Vanya, Oogleen didn't become my papa, but without his help we would still be in Gulja."

"It's amazing that we were both nearly adopted," I said. "I still wonder about my other family. They really loved me."

Misha leaned over and hugged me. "We are your family. Marusia and Lena and I are your family, and Uncle Mitrofan and Aunt Maria are your family."

I felt secure in Misha's embrace and somehow knew I had made the right decision. I slept soundly that evening, not even noticing the unusual noises and foul smells around me.

We arrived in Aksu the next day and were met by Aunt Maria and Dedushka at their apartment. For the next two months, we all lived in Aksu, trying to make a living however we could. Misha taught me how to whitewash walls, which we did together, giving our meager earnings to Aunt Maria. Six days a week we would whitewash, but Sundays were reserved for church. Uncle Mitrofan pastored our small congregation.

Shortly after arriving in Aksu, Misha and I realized the group was preparing to travel to Kashgar, a city some five hundred kilometers to the south. Apparently many of the Russian families felt God was directing them to Kashgar, where they could exit China through India. As I listened to the men debating and praying about this, I couldn't help remembering what Oogleen had said to Misha: "You will never make it out through India. I'll give you permission to go, but I am certain that every one of you will be back in Gulja sooner or later. You wait and see!"

Because I had never actually heard Uncle Mitrofan say that God had spoken to him about Kashgar and India, I questioned whether this was God leading us out through India or just someone's good idea. Whatever the answer, a decision was made.

All of the Russian believers, about ten families, set out for Kashgar in December 1940. The five-hundred-kilometer trip was not as difficult as the trip to Aksu, because there were no mountain passes and glaciers to cross. Each family traveled in wagons that had two large wheels and were pulled by one horse. The trip was very hot and dusty. We traveled along a caravan route known as the Silk Road. I heard our men talk about a Marco Polo who had made this route famous over seven hundred years ago.

We arrived in Kashgar a week later and were stunned by the colorful sights and mysterious sounds of this ancient city. Kashgar is located at the edge of the great Taklimakan Desert and is flanked by the snow-covered Pamirs, some of the highest mountains in the world. Women walked by in tight-fitting, brilliantly patterned dresses with pants underneath. Many of them had long, glistening black braids, some so long they brushed their knees. The red, blue, or green scarves that covered their heads were interwoven with golden thread. Children were everywhere, with little girls parading in dresses even more colorful than those their mothers wore. I quickly noticed that the girls in Kashgar connected their eyebrows with a thin, black line. Misha said they did this to imitate the appearance of Fatima, daughter of Mohammed.

Every morning the city would be saturated by noise, dust, and the distinctive cries of *muezzins* summoning the Muslim men to prayer in the many nearby mosques. Merchants yelled to be heard over the rumbling of hundreds of carts and the braying of thousands of mules. Two-wheeled carts overflowing with fruit, sheep, or children filled the streets. Some were pulled by small horses, others by snorting camels, and still others by tall, bearded men wearing long colorful robes and silver-hilted daggers swinging from their belts. Of the city's many ethnic minorities, the most numerous were the Turkic-speaking Uygurs.

Since none of our Russian and Ukrainian families expected to live in Kashgar very long, we all rented rooms at a caravanserai located right next to the city wall. Our family lived in a large single room with a dirt floor. One of our men was an expert in building Russian ovens, and within a few weeks, every room was outfitted with a Russian oven that served more than just our cooking needs. The top of the oven was used as a bed for the younger children. During the cold winter nights, I would always be curled up atop our oven, enjoying the warmth.

This time in Kashgar was special in that it was the first time I had ever lived with Dedushka, who was quite old and had been cared for by my uncle and aunt since our babushka died. I never knew her. And the only thing I remember Papa saying to us about Dedushka was that he deeply loved God and prayed constantly. In Kashgar I saw firsthand the man's intense faith. Often, as Misha and I would come home from whitewashing, Dedushka would be on his knees, alone, pouring his heart out to God. We would usually stand outside the room and listen to his prayers, not wanting to disturb him. Dedushka always ended his prayers with a plea to God to take him home quickly. He wanted to see God and his wife. But he always insisted that God take him home in such a way that no one would be burdened here on earth.

Dedushka was too old to do any physical work, plus he always had terrible headaches. Misha told me he was sixty-six years old, but I thought he looked older than that. He was always kind to us, and oftentimes as I looked into his eyes, I thought I was talking to Papa. I also could see two deep scars above his eyes and was determined to one day ask where they came from.

Uncle Mitrofan cared for us all like his own children. He reminded me so much of Papa, always loving and kind to me. He never yelled at me. Actually, I don't remember ever hearing him yell at anyone. He was a very godly man, always praying, whether in gratitude for something or seeking answers to puzzling problems. Whenever he was misunderstood by someone at work or at church, Uncle would be the first to ask forgiveness and seek reconciliation. I wanted so much to be like him.

By contrast, I feared Aunt Maria from the day we first arrived at their apartment in Aksu. In many ways, she reminded me of Masha and often treated me with similar harshness. Thankfully I was too old to be beaten, and so I simply had to endure her tongue lashings. Aunt Maria's mean disposition was not directed just toward the four of us but toward everyone. She often treated people unfairly and never asked for forgiveness. Uncle Mitrofan always interceded on Aunt Maria's behalf, begging forgiveness from people hurt by her insensitivity. He always acted kindly toward her, even though she rarely showed any affection and kindness in return. I felt sorry for the way she treated Uncle and often found myself praying for him, asking God to change Aunt Maria.

During the next few months, Misha and I continued whitewashing walls while Uncle Mitrofan worked as a cobbler in a local shoe store. We dutifully handed over all of the money we earned to Aunt Maria, who was very strict and never allowed us to spend any of it on ourselves. To supplement our income, Misha and I would also sell Aunt Maria's baked goods at the local farmers market. Aunt Maria was an excellent baker, and we never came home with leftovers.

Marusia usually stayed home, helping Aunt Maria around the house. Her weakened left hand made it difficult for her to lift heavy objects, though she was one of the hardest workers I knew. I often heard Aunt Maria mumbling under her breath about Marusia being an old maid. Misha told me that if a girl didn't get married between the ages of sixteen and eighteen, she was considered an old maid. Marusia was twenty-one. She was extremely shy and never spoke to boys. I wondered whether her hand had anything to do with that.

One evening during dinner, we heard someone knocking. Marusia jumped up and ran to the door. We could hear the man saying something about a gift for Marusia from . . . and then his voiced trailed off. Marusia walked into the kitchen with a poorly wrapped package.

"What is that?" Aunt Maria demanded.

"It's a gift for me," Marusia replied with delight in her voice.

"Who sent it?" Misha asked.

Marusia, looking down at the floor, answered, "Joseph."

"Who's Joseph?" I asked.

"Hmmph!" Aunt Maria mumbled. "What's that Baptist sending you gifts for?"

"Aren't you going to open it?" Uncle Mitrofan asked, smiling.

"What's a Baptist?" I asked.

Marusia suddenly ripped the package open and pulled out an old sweater. She had a puzzled, almost hurt look on her face as she lifted the sweater up to her chin. Aunt Maria roared with laughter.

"Now that's one ugly sweater!" she yelled, slapping her knee.

Her eyes glistening with tears, Marusia looked at Aunt Maria with deep pain and with something else that I couldn't quite place.

Uncle Mitrofan stood and said, "Maria, stop laughing!" He turned toward Marusia, who was now clutching the sweater against her chest. "Marusia," he began.

"He loves me!" Marusia muttered, still looking at the floor.

Then she looked up at Uncle Mitrofan, tears streaming down her cheeks, and with deep conviction in her voice, she shouted, "And I love him too!"

Uncle stepped toward Marusia, who turned and fled.

"What was that all about?" I asked.

That evening, Misha told me the rest of the story. Joseph Lokteff had first met Marusia five years ago. His parents ran a nylon and sock factory in Gulja. They owned three houses and were much better off than most of the Russians. Joseph hired several of Marusia's girl-friends to do the finish sewing of the toes in the socks. Eventually he asked Marusia to help and then promptly fell head over heels for her. Marusia had never had a boyfriend and approached this relationship with a little skepticism. But soon she, too, fell in love with Joseph.

The problem was with Aunt Maria and some of the church leaders. Joseph attended the Baptist church. Misha then explained that there really wasn't much difference between the Baptists and us, the Pentecostals. The way he saw it, the main difference was how we prayed and what we believed about the Holy Spirit. Otherwise our church services were quite similar. Some of Misha's best friends were Baptists.

"Anyway," Misha continued with the story, "according to Aunt Maria, there was no way that Marusia could marry outside our church. Aunt Maria had done everything possible to end Marusia's relationship with Joseph."

I had often heard Aunt Maria scheming with other women about finding another suitable husband for Marusia. Aunt Maria had even said things like, "How can a normal young man ever marry someone with a crippled arm?" Many times Marusia would be sitting in the next room, listening to all of this. But Marusia had the "I'm in love" look in her eyes, and I noticed her getting more and more bold with Aunt Maria. I couldn't wait to meet this Joseph.

Misha wanted me to learn a profession, and he persuaded Uncle and Aunt to send me to a cobbler's trade school. It was actually a small shoe store owned by a local man who also taught apprentices how to make shoes. Ever since Papa died, I had wanted to learn how to make shoes, to be just like Papa. I began my six-month apprenticeship in July of 1941.

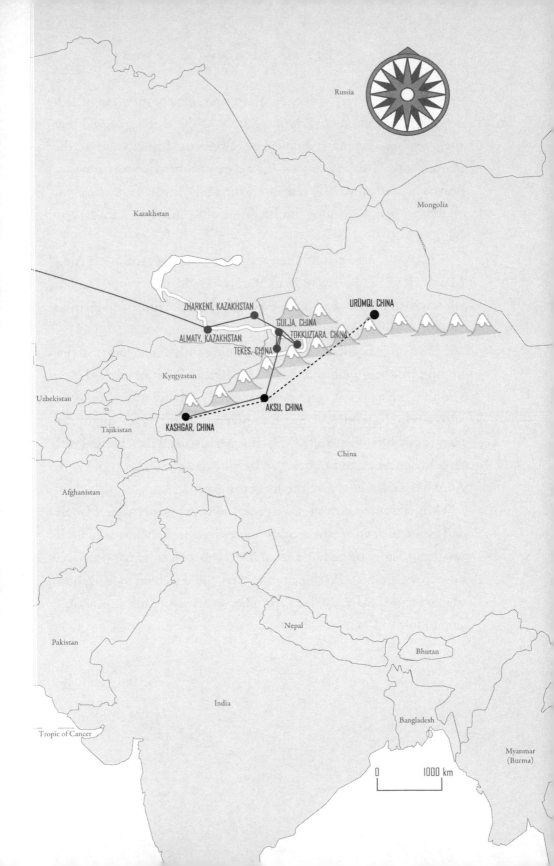

Russia

Mongolia

Kazakhstan

ZHARKENT, KAZAKHSTAN
GULJA, CHINA
URÜMQI, CHINA
ALMATY, KAZAKHSTAN
TOKKUZTARA, CHINA
TEKES, CHINA

Kyrgyzstan

Uzbekistan

Tajikistan

KASHGAR, CHINA
AKSU, CHINA

Afghanistan

China

Pakistan

Nepal

Bhutan

India

Bangladesh

Tropic of Cancer

Myanmar
(Burma)

0   1000 km

THE TOPIC OF leaving through India kept coming up during mealtime conversations and in every prayer meeting Misha and I attended. Some families were openly preparing to leave, but everything changed one strikingly hot December day in 1941.

We were just sitting down to eat our lunch when a loud banging on the front door startled us. As Uncle Mitrofan opened the door, Misha and I crowded next to him to see who it was. An imposing Chinese soldier filled the doorway. Behind him we could see scores of empty two-wheeled wagons.

Before we could ask what the wagons were for, the soldier pulled out a document and thrust it into Uncle Mitrofan's hands. "Gather all your belongings and dump them into one of these wagons," he demanded. "You leave for Gulja tomorrow!"

Aunt Maria rushed to the door, stomping her feet and screaming at the Chinese soldier, "This must be a mistake! How can this be? We can't get ready to leave for Gulja in just one day!"

"Calm down, Maria," Uncle said, placing his hand on her shoulder. Turning to the soldier, he asked, "Where do these orders come from?"

The soldier pointed at the document in Uncle's hand. "It comes from the highest Russian government authority in Gulja."

I glanced over at Misha, and when his eyes met mine, I knew we were thinking the same thing: Oogleen!

Aunt Maria mumbled, and I managed to catch only her last few words: "They want to take us back to Russia!"

Before she could confront the soldier with this thought, Uncle gently but firmly pushed her behind him and addressed the soldier again. "Sir, how can we be expected to leave by tomorrow? We need time to sell our things and prepare food for such a long journey."

"You have no need to worry about anything. You will be provided with enough carts to take all of your belongings. We have orders to purchase as much food as you need for the journey and to provide a military escort that will arrange lodging at caravanserais along the way."

The soldier then stepped back out of our doorway and shouted, "We leave tomorrow at 3:00 PM. Be ready!" After he left, Aunt Maria began ranting and yelling instructions at us all at once.

"Mitrofan, go and find boxes to pack our flour and rice. Misha and Vanya, load these chairs and table onto the wagon. Marusia, the kitchen. O God, why is this happening? How can we be ready by tomorrow? I just know they're going to send us to Russia. My God, what will we do?"

"Maria!" Uncle screamed.

Stunned by Uncle Mitrofan's uncharacteristic show of authority, Aunt Maria stopped crying and focused on Uncle. After an awkward moment of silence, Uncle said as calmly as could be, "Let us pray."

Falling to our knees, our prayers burst forth with desperate urgency. All of us were weeping and pleading to God for direction. Were they going to send us to Russia? Would we be imprisoned again? We needed a word from God, and the word came to Misha.

"He has plotted but will not prevail."

Though we did not fully understand this word, we felt that we had received God's assurance, and we proceeded to prepare ourselves for the long journey ahead.

The next morning, ten families loaded all of their earthly belongings onto twenty-seven wagons. It was an amazing sight. When Misha told me there were twenty-seven wagons, I had to count them for myself, as I had never before seen so many wagons in one place. Until the moment we departed, Aunt Maria kept yelling instructions at us.

Soldiers were at the front and the back of our caravan. An officer in the front motioned for us to move out, and the wagons lurched forward. I was excited about the trip, although my excitement was tempered by a fear of being sent to Russia. As we exited through the eastern gate of the city, I looked back at the high wall surrounding Kashgar. Hundreds of people were waving goodbye to us. I raised my hand and bid them farewell. Soon others in our party were also waving.

The first leg of our trip took us back to Aksu. A journey usually taking less than a week took our caravan a full two weeks. Each family followed the soldiers' instructions to leave nothing behind. As a result, the wagons were overloaded, and the poor horses labored mightily under the strain.

As nightfall approached after our first day of travel, the forward escort galloped ahead to secure housing for us. By the time we got to the caravanserai, all the rooms we needed were ready for us. As we settled in, one of the soldiers said it was time for dinner. Certainly no one expected the banquet that awaited us. Many tables had been set up in a large room, and each table overflowed with tookachi, boiled lamb, dried fruit, melons, and nuts. We supposed the soldiers had been given money to purchase this lavish feast. More incredibly, we were fed in this manner for the entire trip. And every night we ate and celebrated with much thanksgiving and prayer. By the time we arrived in Aksu, our wagons had more bags of rice and flour than when we had started. Thankfully, our escorts allowed us to sell some of our rice and flour to lighten the load of our wagons.

Our escorts knew they could not take us over the Tien Shan glaciers to Gulja, even with our lightened loads. Instead, they led us toward the city of Urümqi on a much longer route around the mountains. For the next six weeks, we traveled through the foothills of the Tien Shan. The soldiers accommodated us in every way. They even secured new wagons for us every 150 kilometers, whether we needed them or not.

Two months after leaving Kashgar, we arrived in Urümqi on February 5, 1942. The city was much bigger than any I'd seen in China, and the streets were crowded with people and livestock. We stayed at a caravanserai just outside the city. As we arrived, I noticed three large army trucks parked outside in a huge field. The canvas flaps in the back were open, revealing their huge cargo areas.

When we came to a halt, the soldier in charge bellowed through his megaphone, "You will have exactly three days to rest here in Urümqi. On the third day at noon, we will leave for Gulja in these trucks."

The soldier then assigned each family to one of the three vehicles. For the next several hours, we all scrambled to transfer belongings into our designated truck. After we finished, Misha said to Uncle and Aunt, "We have three days here in Urümqi. I think I can locate Lena and have her meet us before we leave again. I have letters from her with the address of the school she is attending. It has been eight years since we last saw her. All I need is a little money for the bus."

Aunt Maria became visibly agitated and started protesting. "We don't have enough money as it is, and now you want to throw it away like this. You'll never find her, and besides, you'll probably get lost and not make it back in time."

Misha would not be denied. "Aunt, all I'm asking for is a little of the money Vanya and I earned. You have to let me try to find my little sister. It's been eight years." Then he started to cry.

Uncle put his arm around Misha's shoulder. "Let him go, Maria. Give him enough money to catch a bus to Gulja, just in case he doesn't get back in time."

Aunt Maria scowled as she dug into her purse and plopped some money into Misha's hand. I was so proud of Misha for standing up to Aunt Maria. Though I would have given almost anything to go with him, I knew better than to ask.

During the next two days, I spent every spare moment watching for Misha and Lena. On the third day there was still no sign of Misha, and Aunt Maria began railing at Uncle Mitrofan about how she had told him that Misha would not make it back in time. When the order came to get into the trucks, Uncle pulled me aside and said, "Vanya, let's ask God for a miracle. Maybe He'll help Misha make it back before we leave."

As we prayed, I sensed God's Spirit in a deep way, and I knew He had heard our prayer. The moment we finished praying, we heard the command being given for the trucks to move out. Uncle Mitrofan and I quickly climbed inside our truck, expecting to follow the two trucks that had already sped away. I looked back one last time to see whether Misha and Lena were coming, but I saw no one. Though it looked hopeless, I prayed under my breath. "God, please stop this truck until Misha and Lena get here."

Suddenly the truck's engine stopped. Everyone wondered why we had stopped, and Uncle Mitrofan motioned to me. "Vanya, go find out what's happening."

I jumped out of the truck just as the driver was getting out of the cab. I stepped alongside him and asked why the engine had been turned off. He mumbled something about incorrect documents and walked toward the office. I knew this had to be God, and I ran back to tell Uncle Mitrofan. Giving me a big hug, he said, "God has answered our prayers."

For the next two hours, we sat and waited. I glued my eyes to the bus stop, where I had last seen Misha nearly three days before. Then a bus appeared in the distance. I watched as it wound its way down a dusty hill, making several stops before speeding down the flat stretch of road that led to our caravanserai. When it pulled to a stop, I strained my eyes to see whether anyone got off.

"It's Misha!" I shouted, flying out of the truck and running as fast as I could toward him.

Misha waved and started running toward me. A tall, dark-haired girl followed close behind.

"Misha! I knew you would make it back in time. I knew it! The truck . . . the driver said wrong documents, but I knew it was God."

"Slow down, little brother. Catch your breath!"

Behind him was a girl I barely recognized. She was tall and skinny, with long black hair and deep-set eyes. We stood there silently for a moment just staring at each other.

Breaking the silence, Misha said, "Vanya, this is your sister Lena."

We fell into each other's arms and sobbed tears of joy and sadness, joy that we had found each other again and sadness for the years we had lost.

"Vanyushka, how I've missed you," Lena cried. "Let me have a good look at you. My, how you have grown. I would never have recognized you. How old are you, Vanya?"

"I'm thirteen years old," I replied in a voice still choked with emotion.

By then Uncle Mitrofan, Aunt Maria, and Marusia had run up to us, and they, too, showered Lena with hugs and kisses and many tears.

We knew we had precious little time for catching up with our long-lost sister. Lena told us of her desire to study medicine and to one day become a family doctor. As we were heading back to the truck, the driver was coming out of the office.

"We probably have to leave soon," I said, motioning toward the driver.

At that, Misha ran ahead and, explaining that we had just found our sister, asked if we could spend more time with her.

"You have forty-five minutes," he said. "Then the truck is leaving."

As the driver turned and walked back to the office, our family began hugging Lena again.

Right before it came time to leave, Misha persuaded Aunt and Uncle to give more of our money to Lena so she could possibly visit us in Gulja. Lena kept saying that it was like a dream—she could hardly believe her family was together again. As the truck pulled away, her dark eyes filled with tears once more.

"Thank you for finding me, Misha. I love you all."

I couldn't stop crying. I looked back at Lena until she disappeared in the dusty horizon.

"God," I prayed, "please let me see my sister again."

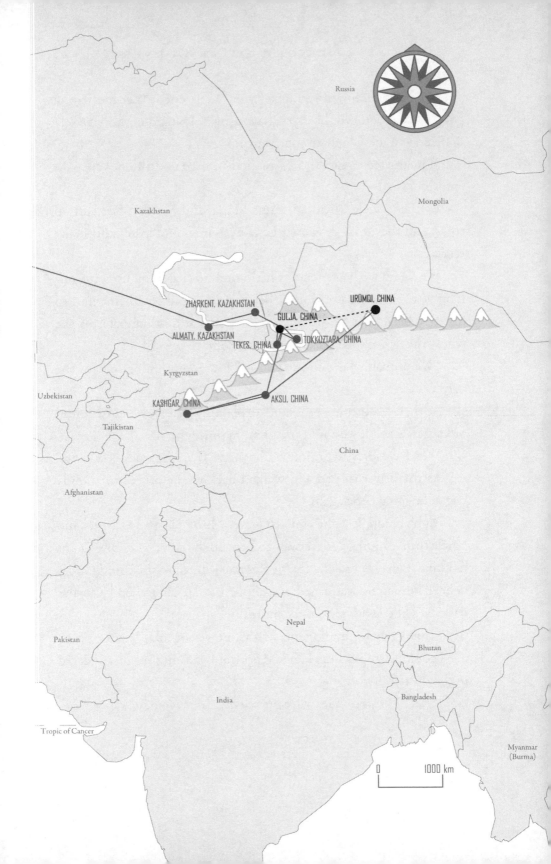

ELEVEN

THE TWO TRUCKS ahead of us were long gone. Because many in our group expressed concern about being taken back to Russia, we spent a lot of time in the truck praying and singing hymns as we lumbered down the road. Our leaders said there was an important fork in the road at a town called Wusu. If the truck turned north, we were heading to Russia. If it continued westward, it meant we were going to Gulja. Our prayers grew more fervent the closer we got to Wusu. Suddenly we heard a loud noise, and the truck swerved violently to the left. Hearing a thumpity-thump noise, we realized our left rear tire had just blown.

There we were, less than a kilometer away from this important fork in the road, and we still didn't know which way our truck would turn. At that moment, I recalled the word God had given Misha earlier, and I felt reassured that He would guide our truck to Gulja.

Once the driver had replaced the tire, we set off again. As we approached Wusu, the truck seemed to veer slightly to the right, but

Thailand

Philippines

at the last moment it turned westward toward Gulja. Our prayers turned into joyous singing and praise.

On the fourth and final day of our journey from Urümqi, our truck labored up the narrow, potholed road over the Talki Mountains. Atop the pass was a large, deep-blue lake called Sairam. Given its beauty, I was surprised to hear Uncle say it was dead and salty with no fish in it. After we passed the lake, the road down the mountain became steep and windy. Our driver stopped several times to cool our brakes and give us time to rest. I was glad our driver was so cautious. This narrow pass was no place to lose your brakes. Finally, after a bumpy and dusty day of travel, we made our way to the valley below and saw the familiar sights of Gulja.

We were greeted by several Christian families, including the Shevchenkos. I ran up to Alex and hugged him. Since the last time I had seen him, he had married and had several children. He introduced us to his family, and his parents invited us to live with them until we could find our own place. All of us were still concerned about being sent back to Russia, but we heard nothing from the authorities. We began looking for work and trying to resume our lives in Gulja.

After living with the Shevchenkos for a week, Uncle and Aunt found an apartment for rent. The apartment had two large rooms divided by a long hallway. We lived in one room, and the Zhernovy family took the other. The Zhernovys had four daughters, and their youngest, Lily, was around my age.

Since Uncle, Aunt, Dedushka, my brother, my sister, and I had traveled so much together, we had grown accustomed to sharing a single room, and thus we were able to arrange our common living space in a way that was satisfactory to all. Uncle and Aunt draped a sheet beside their bed, and Misha and I slept on the other side, along with Dedushka. Marusia made her bed near the door.

Aunt Maria continued to yell at us for the smallest things. She also treated Dedushka unkindly, maybe because she had a hard time taking care of him. I didn't think he was a burden, and I always looked forward to his company. Dedushka grew weary of Aunt Maria's unkindness and often let her know it. Every day, he would pour out his complaints to God in prayer.

The thing Aunt Maria hated most was Dedushka's loud snoring. Many times, she would get up in the middle of the night, poke Dedushka on the shoulder, and tell him to stop snoring. After a loud gulp, he would always say, "Ah, oh, it's you bothering me again. Just you wait till you get to be my age. Now let me be and let me sleep."

His snoring bothered me, too, but I tried to be more understanding. One night I poked him myself just to see if he would yell at Aunt Maria. When he did, I nearly choked with laughter.

Since we had started living together, I had wanted to ask Dedushka about the scars on his forehead. We happened to be alone at home one afternoon, and I mustered up the courage to ask. He looked at me with tired eyes. "It's a long story, Vanya. Are you sure you want to hear all of it?"

"Yes, I do!"

Sitting down at the table, Dedushka smiled at me. "How about if I first tell you a story about your papa and mama and then about these scars?"

"Please do, Dedushka."

"Your papa and Mitrofan were my only sons. My wife—your babushka—and I raised them in the Orthodox Church, though none of us really knew much about God. It was your uncle Mitrofan who first became a Christian, and then my wife and I accepted God into our lives. But your father's and mother's conversions were a little different.

"Yakov was earnest and sincere in all his ways, and he accepted what Mitrofan told him about God. When he told Pelageya, your mother, that he was no longer an Orthodox believer, she immediately told this to Matthew Gradovsky, her father. Christians who were not part of the Orthodox denomination were called sectarians at that time, and her father, a devout Orthodox believer, was incensed that Yakov had joined a Christian sect.

"Pelageya asked her father what she should do to get Yakov back into the Orthodox Church. He instructed her to publicly humiliate Yakov whenever she had a chance. So every time your father would bow his knees to pray, your mother would walk up behind him with a pail of pig slop and dump it on his head!"

"How disgusting!" I blurted. Scooting closer to Dedushka, I asked, "But what did Papa do every time Mama emptied that pail on his head?"

"Your Papa was a humble and patient man. He would go to the church leaders, tell them what happened, and ask for wisdom. They always said to continue praying for more patience. And how your papa prayed, because he needed lots of patience! You see, this went on for nearly three months."

I could scarcely believe my ears. Incredulously, I said, "You mean Mama dumped that pig slop on Papa's head every day for three months?"

Dedushka smiled. "Every day. For three months, your papa had to wash off the pig slop every time he prayed."

"But how did Mama change? When did she stop doing this and become a Christian? Did Papa—"

"Calm down, Vanya!" Dedushka said, leaning over and patting me on the head. I was all worked up and wanted to know how my mother could have been so mean.

"After three months, your mama was getting frustrated because your papa would not come back to the Orthodox faith. So once again off she went to her father's house and asked for more advice.

"'What's Yakov doing right now?' her father asked.

"'He's attending a prayer meeting at their church building,' your mother replied.

"'Then you go to that prayer meeting with a large stick and beat him and try to humiliate him as much as you can,' was her father's advice."

"Did Mama really do this?" I asked.

Dedushka rubbed the scars on his forehead and replied, "Oh yes. Your mama did exactly what her father told her to do. She found a large piece of discarded lumber, walked into the church building, and raised the stick high over her head, ready to strike your papa."

"But . . . but she didn't hit Papa, did she?"

"Well, Vanya, something amazing happened," Dedushka said, rubbing his hands together in anticipation of what he was about say.

"You see, I was at that prayer meeting and saw it all. When Pelageya walked in, only a few of us noticed her. Everybody else was lost in prayer. I noticed her dragging in that large piece of wood and knew that she was up to no good. The look on her face also gave her away. When she raised that big stick above your papa's head, several of us thought of trying to stop her, but no one moved. We just watched as a miracle unfolded right before our eyes.

"Pelageya suddenly began to cry, and the mean look on her face melted away. Her hands started shaking, and that huge piece of wood came crashing to the floor. It was almost as if someone had knocked it out of her hands. When the piece of wood fell, Yakov and the rest of our group, startled by the noise, looked up at Pelageya. I will remember the look on Yakov's face till the day I die."

Dedushka looked up at a picture of Papa and Mama hanging on our wall and sighed.

"Dedushka, what happened next?"

"Well," he continued, looking back at me, "Pelageya looked stunned, like someone had struck her on the head. Probably the Holy Spirit, if you ask me. Anyway, Yakov leapt to his feet and shouted, 'Pelageya! What are you doing here?'

"Your mama had a broken look on her face, and she said, 'I don't know what's happening to me. I came here to humiliate you, but I can't go through with it. I feel so rotten for the way I've treated you over these past three months. I feel dirty. Yakov, I want what you have. I want God.'

"Yakov started weeping and embraced your mama. Then the entire group surrounded them and began praying. They must have prayed for them for over an hour. And that's how your mama came to Jesus."

I looked up at the picture of Papa and Mama and stared at it for a long time. How I missed them, even after so many years. As I wiped my teary eyes with my sleeve, I noticed Dedushka rubbing his head— then I remembered his scars.

"Dedushka, you promised to tell me about your scars."

"It happened long ago, when we were still living in Ukraine," Dedushka began. "I think it was around 1932, and we were living in Adamovka, the village where your papa and mama were born. Mitrofan and Maria had already moved to Tashkent, and Yakov had taken his family to Baku.

"Mitrofan sent us a letter urging us to join him in Tashkent, and after much prayer, we agreed to go. I sold our house for about three thousand rubles. Right before we were to move out, I received the money and hid the bulk of it under one of the loose floorboards. And I placed about seventy rubles into a jar next to the bed.

"That evening, as we were sleeping, I was awakened by a loud noise. It sounded like a barrel crashing to the floor. Your babushka also heard it and said she was going to see what it was. As she got out of bed, I reached for a match and followed her toward the bedroom door. As she opened the door, I struck the match. What happened next was an absolute nightmare."

Dedushka's eyes welled up with tears, and his lip started quivering. I reached out and took his hands in mine and gave him a reassuring squeeze.

"It happened so quickly, almost like a blur. But I noticed their faces before someone blew out my match. All I could hear was Babushka screaming as they strangled her. I started flailing my arms and yelling, hoping someone outside would hear me. Then somebody pushed me backward and began beating me with what I think was a pipe. Babushka's screams grew weaker and weaker, and then I couldn't hear her anymore.

"After that, both men continued beating me. They kicked me, pulled my beard out in clumps, and slammed my head against the floor, yelling, 'Where's the money? We know you sold this house. Now where is it?'

"Scared as I was, I decided to reveal only where the seventy rubles were, not the money hidden under the floorboard. They went to grab the money and came back more furious than before.

"'This isn't all of it, old man. Tell us where the rest is, or we'll kill you!'

"I knew they had killed your babushka—I saw it in their faces— and that they were likely going to kill me too. I felt like I had nothing more to lose, so I didn't tell them where the rest of the money was. All I remember after that is the way they beat my head against the floor and kicked me. I must have passed out, because the next thing I remember is opening my eyes and feeling a heavy weight on top of me. I found it nearly impossible to breathe, and my body was aching all over. I tried to move, but my hands were tied behind my back. I was lying facedown, and I tried to turn enough so whatever was on top of me would slide off. To my surprise, I managed to squirm out from under it.

"I could finally breathe again, but something was blurring my vision. I slowly got to my feet. The robbers had torn open our bed and dumped it on top of me. I rubbed my eyes on the bed and noticed blood all over my shirt. I was bleeding from the wounds to my head, and I knew I needed to get help fast. Then I heard a noise outside. Someone was calling for me and Babushka.

"Stumbling out of the bedroom, I almost tripped over my dear wife. I fell to my knees and called her name several times, hoping she was still breathing. But the closer I got to her, the more I realized she wasn't alive anymore. They had murdered her."

Then Dedushka and I both started to cry. We held each other, grieving for the love that he had lost.

I had one more question that kept nagging at me, and I had to ask it. I peeked up at his face and asked softly, "Did you tell the police who did it?"

Dedushka shook his head and sighed deeply.

"I knew exactly who did it, but when the police questioned me, I didn't tell them anything. Why create even more problems for my relatives, I thought. My wife was dead, and nothing was going to bring her back. Especially not revenge or bitterness."

Dedushka rubbed his scars again and looked away. I stood up and threw my arms around his neck and squeezed him as hard as I could, gently caressing his scars.

"Thanks, Grandfather!" I whispered in his ear. "I love you!"

That was to be the last story Dedushka ever told me. A few months later he went to bed and never woke up.

PART 3

JANUARY 1942—GULJA

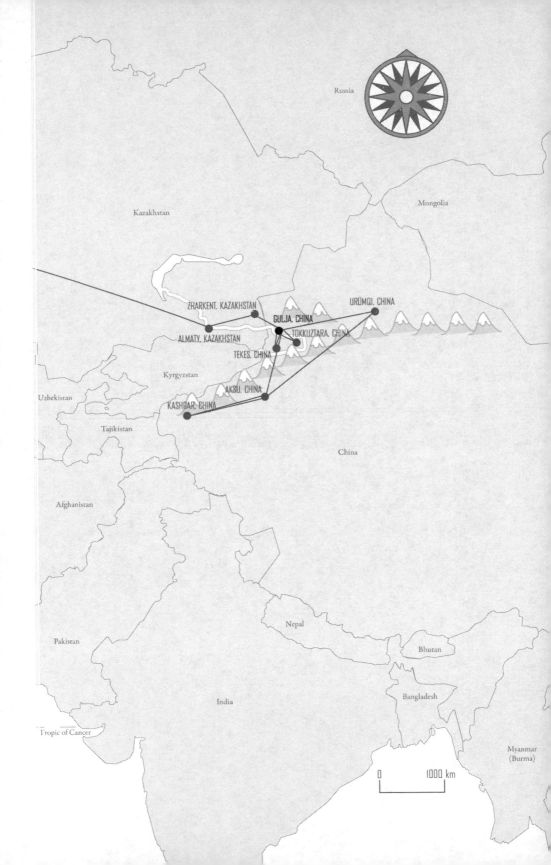

N GULJA our lives seemed far removed from the great battles going on in the rest of the world in early 1942. We heard little about this Second World War. We knew Russia was allied with America and England against the Nazis of Germany. And in the east, Japan had invaded China, Korea, and Southeast Asia. We also heard about a Chinese revolutionary army led by someone named Mao. Both Russian and Chinese soldiers operated in and around Gulja, and I never knew who was really in control. We hoped the war in Russia and China kept them so occupied that they wouldn't bother to deport us.

Shortly after we arrived, Misha got a job in maintenance at the local airport. He also fell in love with Nadya Vodopyanova, and they spent a lot of time together. Because our pastor and elders were constantly instructing us young people about the perils of lust, we were never permitted to be alone with the opposite sex. Boys and girls were permitted to meet with each other only in groups. We were told this would protect us from the temptation to sin.

Marusia wanted to become a seamstress and convinced Aunt Maria to allow her to study at a local shop. I wondered whether this had something to do with Joseph, whom I had already met several times. I could tell that Marusia really liked him, and I liked him too. Joseph was an excellent musician and an exceptional choir director. I didn't quite understand why Aunt Maria didn't like him; I thought he would make a great husband for Marusia.

One day Joseph came to our house, but instead of wanting to see Marusia, he asked to speak to Uncle Mitrofan. Misha and I crept up to the door to hear their conversation.

"I . . . I would like to . . . to speak with you a . . . about Marusia," Joseph stammered.

"Alright," Uncle Mitrofan said.

"I love Marusia and would like to ask you for her hand in marriage," said Joseph, who suddenly sounded sure of himself and didn't stammer.

"You would like to marry Marusia?" Uncle Mitrofan questioned.

"Yes, I would."

"I will agree under one condition," Uncle Mitrofan replied. "That she not be married in your church."

"But why?" Joseph sounded shocked and crushed.

Misha and I could hear Uncle pushing his chair away from the table. The conversation was over. Misha beckoned me to follow him as he turned and ran outside. We watched Joseph shuffle away, shoulders drooped and with a puzzled look on his face.

Several weeks later, we heard Marusia say that Joseph fell ill and requested the wedding be postponed. Aunt Maria, emboldened by this postponement, tried desperately to get Marusia to marry Alex

Mahovski. Alex and his parents attended our church, and I often saw him at youth meetings. Alex was quite short and pudgy and even more shy than Marusia. Aunt Maria started inviting Alex and his parents over for dinner, always seating Marusia right next to Alex. But Marusia did not like Alex. She would always ask Aunt if Joseph could come for dinner, but the answer was always the same: "No!"

One day I overheard Marusia's conversation with Aunt Maria.

"Because you are just a poor orphan with a crippled hand. That's why you need to marry Alex," Aunt Maria fumed.

"But I don't love him!" Marusia exclaimed.

"What does love have to do with this?" Aunt Maria shouted. "You live in my house, under my roof. You don't have a choice in this matter."

"I will not marry Alex," an emboldened Marusia replied. "Joseph will come for me. God told me so."

I was stunned by Marusia's boldness. And I didn't have to wait too long to see the results.

Less than a week later, Misha met me as I came bounding through the door. "Have you heard about Marusia?" Misha said.

"No," I said expectantly. "What happened?"

"She's getting married!" shouted Misha with a big, wide grin on his face.

"Please don't say she's marrying Alex," I retorted.

"She's marrying Joseph, her prince, who came and stole her away on a wagon!"

And out came the story. Since Aunt Maria was no longer allowing Joseph to visit Marusia at our home, one day, a week or so earlier, Nadya Vodopyanova had come for a visit. Aunt Maria didn't suspect anything and was not at all concerned when Nadya asked Marusia to step outside. Unbeknownst to Aunt Maria, Joseph's friend was waiting in a wagon for Marusia. Nadya literally pushed Marusia into the wagon, and away they rode as fast as possible.

One block from the house, Joseph joined Marusia in the wagon, and they darted off to the marriage registration office. Within an hour they were legally registered to get married and had set a date for their wedding: April 4, 1942.

Marusia married Joseph in a wonderful ceremony held at Joseph's house. Aunt Maria did not attend the wedding, though Uncle Mitrofan did. Both Misha and I were in the wedding. The couple were married by Ionko, the assistant pastor of our Pentecostal church. Then, two weeks later, on April 25, Misha and Nadya also got married. Suddenly I was once again living alone with Uncle and Aunt, but I was very happy for my older brother and sister.

I decided to continue learning the cobbler's trade. Uncle Mitrofan was a good cobbler, and he specialized in making boots. I spent many hours watching and learning as he made each boot by hand. But rather than just teach me to make boots, Uncle wanted me to attend an established training program where I could learn to design and cut out patterns for shoes. Then, he said, we could work together.

Misha also wanted me to continue my training and persuaded Aunt to let me attend a thirty-month cobbler's apprenticeship program. He even promised to help pay for part of my training with his own earnings. And so, shortly after his wedding, I began my apprenticeship. The school was run by Foon Svo, a Russian-speaking Chinese master cobbler who had studied his craft in Vladivostok, Russia. Foon Svo's assistant, Chee Svo, also came from Russia. Their school had sixteen students and was split between two sites: the preparatory site, or the shoe store, and the site where they made the soles. Since I had some experience, I, along with seven other students, worked at the shoe store.

When customers would order a certain style of shoe, Chee Svo would cut the shoe pattern out of leather and give it to me. I would then bend and glue all the ends, preparing it to be sewn onto the sole. Only the master was allowed to use the one industrial sewing machine we had, but within nine months Foon Svo had me doing all the sewing work for the shop.

Foon Svo liked me from the start, and because of my honesty, he placed me in charge of the students. Whenever there was a fracas among the students, Foon Svo and Chee Svo would first ask me what happened. They would always believe me over what any other student would say. We all lived together in a crude dormitory during the week and were allowed to visit family on the weekends. Though my faith in God was strong, it was tested, especially during that first year.

Most of my fellow apprentices were Chinese. My closest friends were two brothers, Vanya and Kolya Kopeykin. Though their parents went to church, the brothers weren't that interested in God. Neither were the three other Russian apprentices: Viktor, Paul, and Efrim. In the evenings all six of us began hanging out together, and my troubles began on one such evening.

Right before dinner, the apprentices were commenting that the food in our big communal pot didn't look edible. Kolya came up with an enticing alternative.

"Let's go to the market and steal some watermelons."

"Now that's a great idea!" Viktor said, slapping me on the back. "Come on, Vanya, let's go have some fun."

The guys started to get up when I spoke up.

"No!" I exclaimed. "I'm a Christian, and it's wrong to steal."

"Oh, come on *baba*!" Viktor said. "Do something fun for once in your life!" All the others started laughing and slapping me on the back.

"I can't steal!" I said as forcefully as I knew how.

"Okay, that's fine," Kolya replied. "Come along and act like you're buying the watermelon, and we'll do the stealing."

I knew this was still not right, but I rationalized that I wouldn't be stealing the watermelon, just eating it.

I have to admit the watermelon tasted good. I felt a pang of guilt when I ate it, but I brushed the feeling off. The second time was a little easier, and by the time a month had rolled by, we were stealing melons three times a week. I didn't steal them. I just distracted the seller so my friends could steal them. This went on for about four months. When I attended church services, I sometimes felt slight pangs of guilt, but once I was back with my friends, the guilty feelings would quickly disappear.

One Saturday evening as I arrived home, I found Uncle sharing the gospel with a university student named Mitya Chirkoff. I had seen Mitya before but, because of the age difference, had never spoken to him. I sat quietly, listening intently to everything Uncle said. He told Mitya about how Jesus had come to give His life for him and that the only way to heaven was through Him. He said we must repent of our sins because God is righteous and holy and no unredeemed sinner will be allowed into heaven.

Then Uncle began talking to Mitya about the judgment day, about how God cannot tolerate sin. He said all sin hurts God and creates havoc in our lives. Only through repentance and the blood of Jesus can we receive new life.

As I listened, I started feeling those pangs of guilt again, only much stronger. I felt as if Uncle was speaking directly to me. I began to sweat and squirm. Something inside me wanted to cry out, to repent, to acknowledge my hypocrisy. *I can't go on living a lie. I have to do something. I need to change. I need to confess my sin. O God, please help me!*

Just then, Mitya got up and shook hands with Uncle. "Thank you for telling me all this. I would like to take some time to think about all you said. Maybe we can speak again soon."

As Mitya walked out the door, I suddenly cried out, "Uncle! Enough! I can't go on like this anymore."

"Vanya, what's the matter? Are you sick?" Uncle looked frightened as he stepped forward and stared into my eyes.

"Uncle, I can't keep living like this. You think I'm a good Christian boy, but I'm not." Tears were pouring down my cheeks. My voice was trembling, and I could barely speak. "I feel so rotten, so filthy. I'm a liar and a thief. We stole watermelons, and I ate them. I did it with my friends for over four months. I can't go on like this. Uncle, please pray and ask God to forgive me."

I couldn't contain my grief anymore. Like a dam it burst, and I fell to my knees, sobbing and begging God for forgiveness. Uncle didn't quite know what was happening, but he placed his hands on me and began calling out to God as I prayed for forgiveness.

"O God," I cried, "forgive me for lying and stealing. I make a commitment today never again to lie or steal. I recommit my life to You."

God's conviction of my sin was very strong. I will never forget how good I felt after receiving His forgiveness. My feelings of guilt disappeared, and I felt free and clean.

As we stood from prayer, Uncle Mitrofan looked at me through tear-filled eyes and said, "This is a very important time in your life, Vanya. Whatever promises you make to God, you must take very seriously."

"Uncle, I promised God I will pray every morning and evening in my dorm room in front of my peers, no matter what they say. And I will never again participate in stealing watermelons."

Little did I know how difficult it would be to keep my promises. That next evening after returning to my dorm, I quickly got ready to go to sleep. All the other boys were crawling into their beds, talking loudly about all they had done the past two days. I was determined to get on my knees and pray loudly, when suddenly a strange thing happened. I couldn't move. It was as if I was glued to my bed. I shuffled my feet and began sweating profusely. I tried pushing myself off the bed and onto my knees, but something was holding me back.

Meanwhile, I could hear my friends talking about stealing watermelons again. I knew they were going to talk to me soon. Right then I lurched forward and fell to my knees and cried out as loud as I could, "O God, I love You! Help me serve You daily. Forgive me for stealing watermelons, and I promise never to steal again."

I could almost feel my friends' stares on the back of my head as the room became deathly still. My body was shaking, and sweat was pouring down my face. And then it began. I recognized Viktor's voice as he mocked me. "Ho—ly man! We have a genuine holy man in our midst!"

Viktor's pillow glanced off my head as the rest of the boys chimed in with their deriding cries. I could feel pillows hitting me on my back and head as the room erupted in mocking laughter. Everyone was yelling, and pillows were flying at me from every corner of the room.

But I had done it. I had kept my promise to pray out loud. Eventually the laughter stopped and the pillows disappeared. I started and ended each day on my knees, just as I had promised God.

For the next year or so, my friends continued to taunt me about joining in on their stealing binges, but I refused. And because I was well-liked and trusted by my two bosses, my peers were not able to intimidate me too much.

When I finished my apprenticeship in August 1944, I worked as a master cobbler alongside Foon Svo and Chee Svo for several months. Then I found a job with Hong Che, a wonderful Chinese cobbler who owned a small shop several kilometers from Gulja.

During my second month with Hong Che, the war finally made its way to our little corner of the world. It was strange because Russia and China were supposedly allies in the war against Japan. But along their border, tensions had been growing. The fighting in our area was referred to as the Turkestanskaya War, although I never did fully understand why this war had broken out. What little I knew came from comments by the older men in our church. They said the Russian government had fomented a revolution ten years earlier in Sinkiang. Now the Chinese army under General Chiang Kai-shek was forcing all the Russians out of positions of power in Sinkiang and other border areas, killing many outright. The Chinese military took up strategic positions in Urümqi and Gulja, including Seeleemboo, a fort in the old part of Gulja.

Our church leaders said the Russians responded by agitating the Uygurs and Dungans against the Chinese. We heard rumors that an underground army, led by a Russian military commander named Leskin, was being formed. This army grew quickly because Russian boys ages twelve years and up were being forced to join. The Russians were mobilizing in our area expressly to take the Seeleemboo fort back from the Chinese.

As the war escalated, Chinese citizens were being killed daily. I was shocked to hear that my friends Foon Svo and Chee Svo were among the dead. I couldn't understand why the Russian soldiers would kill men who had helped so many Russian boys. Each time I thought of it, my eyes welled with tears. My new boss, Hong Che, was forced by Russians to work for their soldiers. He was taken so suddenly that he had no chance to pay me for my last month of work. I decided to visit him, wanting to make sure he was alive.

When I arrived, Hong Che was shocked to see me and begged my forgiveness for not paying me. I assured him that was not why I had come. He was clearly afraid, and after I expressed my concern for his life, he settled down. I then prayed for him and left.

In mid-October of 1944 the army came looking for me. Most of the time, soldiers just grabbed boys right off the streets. These soldiers knocked on our door and forced me to go with them. As I was leaving, Uncle and Aunt said they would be praying all day for me, trusting God to deliver me. I was herded into a large military truck along with scores of other boys my age and younger. We were taken to a large field near the outskirts of town, now covered with green army tents and hundreds of scared recruits. After filling out a questionnaire, I found myself in a long line of boys awaiting their posting. I could see a tall military officer at the head of the line ordering each boy where he was to go.

The boys around me were all talking about the impending battle for Seeleemboo. There was a tangible fear among them. Many cried openly; others prayed that God would keep them from being killed in battle.

Meanwhile, the line was moving forward, and I could see the Russian officer who was giving orders. He looked huge and terrifying, especially with his shiny Mauser pistol at his side. With the flick of his finger and without any noticeable emotion, he was sending twelve-year-old boys to war. My mind was racing, and I prayed silently for help.

What should I say to him, Lord? If I'm sent to the front, I may never come back alive. Then a thought popped into my mind. *I'll tell him my religious convictions do not allow me to take a rifle and kill people. That's it! That's what I'll tell him.*

I felt sure this was what God wanted me to say. Soon I was staring right into the officer's stern, chiseled face. As the officer looked at me, his voice boomed, "And what do you have to say for yourself, young man?"

My mouth opened, and these words jumped out: "Sir, I'm not sure what I'm doing here. You see, I'm too young to be here."

"Do you have documents with you?" he snapped.

"Yes sir," I replied as I handed over the document I had just picked up at the local government office. The officer grabbed it out of my hands and glanced over it quickly. Then he started shouting, "How could they be such buffoons!"

I could scarcely believe what I was seeing as I saw him take a red pen out of his desk and scrawl right across my document the words "Send him home!"

"Here, show this document to those fools and go home." He shoved the document into my hands and turned toward the next boy in line.

I was stunned! *God,* I thought, *You put those words into my mouth. You delivered me.* Then I recalled what Uncle and Aunt had told me as I was leaving home.

I ran up to the two officers processing our orders and showed them my document. They were truly baffled as they both scrutinized my document.

"How could this be?" they asked. "You're fifteen years old. Why in the world is he sending you home?"

I didn't say a word as I watched them agonize over my orders. But they finally said, "He's our commander, and we can't disobey his orders. You're free to go."

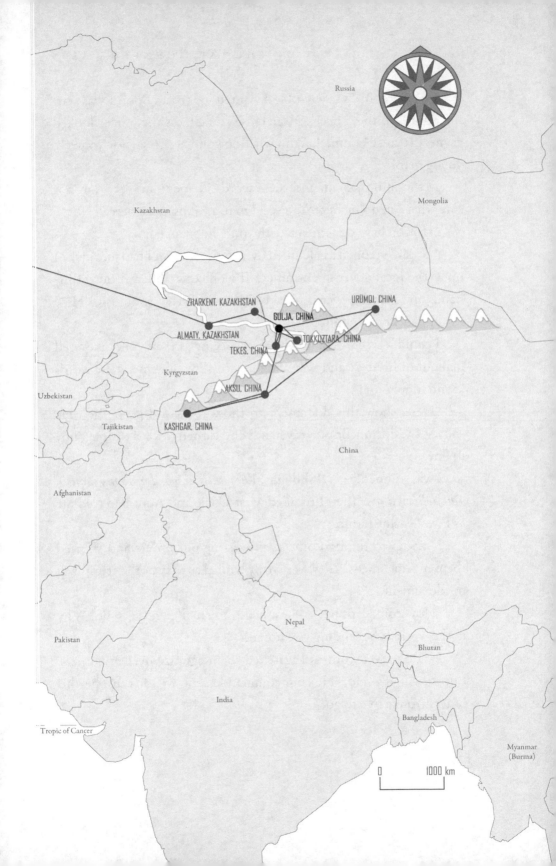

THIRTEEN

I RAN ALL THE WAY HOME, bursting through our front door, huffing and puffing. I was surprised to find a room full of people on their knees praying. They looked up at me, and then with a collective shout they all rushed toward me, hugging and patting me on the head.

"I was sent home," I said as I hugged Uncle.

"We knew you would be," Uncle replied, so matter-of-factly that I was taken aback. "God spoke to us in prayer and assured us you would not be sent to the front but would come home today. We've been expecting you."

God had truly delivered me from almost certain death. Over the next several months, the battle for Seeleemboo waged hot and furious. Many of Russia's boy soldiers died in the fighting. The main battle took place in December, and by the new year the fort was taken back by the Russians. The winter was so severe that many Chinese soldiers froze as they were evacuating. Dead bodies were strewn throughout the city, especially in and around the fort. Had I been sent to the front in October, only God knows whether I would have survived.

My exemption from military service was short-lived, however. In January 1945 two soldiers came knocking on our door. This time I could say nothing as they led me directly to the main military barracks in the center of the city. After filling out the appropriate paperwork, I waited for my orders. Several officers walked by, but only one stopped and spoke to me.

"What's your name, son?"

His question startled me as I jumped to my feet and stood at attention.

"Vanya Yakovich Iliyn, sir."

"And what's your profession, Vanya Yakovich?"

"I'm a master cobbler, sir."

"How many years' experience do you have?"

"Three years, five months, sir."

"Do you know how to cut out patterns and use an industrial sewing machine?"

His questions indicated some knowledge of the cobbler's trade. I answered, "That's my specialty, sir."

"I see," he said, rubbing his chin. I could see by his uniform that he was a major. His name tag said Beardin.

"At ease, Vanya Yakovich." He then turned around and left.

I didn't have long to ponder this strange encounter, because two soldiers appeared and ordered me to follow them. I was led into a long barracks full of rickety bunk beds.

"The top one is your bunk," one of the soldiers said as he shoved an assault rifle into my chest. "And here's your rifle. Make sure to keep it clean."

I refused to take it.

"What's your problem?" he asked, staring at me in disbelief.

"I'm sorry, but I can't take the rifle. You see, I'm a Christian and my faith doesn't permit me to kill others."

As I was talking, more soldiers began listening.

"This is an army! You don't have a choice!" The two soldiers started to throw the rifle at me. I kept my hands behind my back, and the rifle almost fell to the floor before one of them caught it. Within a few moments, I was surrounded by other sneering soldiers yelling obscenities at me for refusing to take the rifle.

In my heart I was calling out to God for courage. The atmosphere was charged with so much hatred that I knew violence could break out any minute.

"Don't let him get away with this!"

"Yeah, he's nothing more than a sissy!"

"Let's wrap the rifle around his neck!"

The circle was closing in around me when suddenly I felt the rifle hanging around my neck. The barracks began rocking as the soldiers stomped their feet and yelled themselves into a frenzy.

O God! I silently prayed. *Help me.*

I expected to be kicked and beaten at any moment. Then the room fell silent. One of the two original soldiers raised his hand and quieted the barracks as he spoke.

"You're not going to get away with this," he sneered. "I don't care about your faith in God. You're in the army now, and you will take orders!"

His nostrils flared, and his face turned red as he spoke. His veins were pulsating in his neck. As he spoke, he leaned so close to my face I could almost taste his anger.

"Are you afraid to die?" he whispered to me.

"No, I'm not," I replied emphatically as I folded my arms across my chest.

"Good," he continued. "Because I'm going to recommend to our superior officer that you be made an example to all other soldiers of what will happen if they disobey."

Then he turned to all the soldiers and shouted, "Let's have him shot by a firing squad!"

The barracks exploded in a maniacal tide of anger. Soldiers were screaming and kicking their bunk beds as they anticipated my execution. Some began swarming around me again, punching at my head and hurling vile insults. Suddenly I felt someone grabbing my hands and yanking them behind me. I could feel the rope bite into my flesh as it was tightened around my wrists. I tried turning around to see who was doing this, when everything went dark. For a second I was completely disoriented. Then I realized I was being blindfolded. As soon as the blindfold was secured, the soldiers cheered like rowdy soccer fans celebrating their team's winning goal.

Amidst all this frenzy, I began to feel as though I were inside a peaceful cocoon. It was almost as if I had found one of my beloved dark corners, where no one could harm me, where I was alone with my thoughts and with God. Here I was, on the verge of being shot by the firing squad, and I was totally at peace with God and with myself.

"God," I whispered, "if this be Your will, I'm ready to die. Maybe this is where my life ends and I finally get to see Papa and Mama and You in heaven. Just one bullet and I'll be with You."

An unearthly joy seemed to wash over me. Not only was I ready to die, but also I found myself saying to God, "Take me now. I look forward to that bullet."

The next thing I knew, I was being shoved away from the crowd into a corner. My blindfold was yanked off, and I found myself staring into the face of our commanding officer.

The soldiers were screaming even louder now. "Execute him! Make an example of him! No mercy!"

The commander raised his hand and shouted, "Quiet!"

The barracks instantly went still, with all the soldiers standing at attention yet slightly leaning toward me with their ears perked.

"What's this all about, Iliyn?" he asked.

"Sir, I'm completely at your mercy. You can do whatever you wish with me. I'm willing to do anything for you except take up the rifle."

The commander smirked. "You know I can send you to the front without your rifle, and you would probably not last more than a day?"

"Yes, you can, sir," I said, "but that will not change my convictions. I can die in the field or before a firing squad. Either way, sir, I'm not afraid to die."

The soldiers around me stirred but said nothing in obvious fear of our commander. As I glanced upward, the commander was stroking his walrus mustache and staring out the window. With just a flick of his hand, I knew I could be sent to my death. Yet I felt no dread. I knew God was the One who ultimately held my life in His hands.

Then the commander turned toward the soldiers. "Listen up! Forget the firing squad. I'll take care of Vanya by sending him to the front without his rifle. Let the Chinese kill him. That ought to teach him and anybody else who disobeys orders a lesson. Dismissed!"

The commander grabbed me by my shoulders as the other soldiers dispersed.

"Iliyn, you think I won't send you to the front?"

"Quite the contrary, sir. I know you have the authority to put me in front of a firing squad or to send me to the front without a rifle. I'm at your mercy."

He glowered at me. "Be ready to leave for the front at 0600 tomorrow." He abruptly spun to his left and marched out of the room.

I watched as he left, and from the corner of my eye I spotted the head of another officer standing near the door. I couldn't tell who it was, but I did wonder how long he had been standing there. He walked up to my commander and began conversing with him. The few of us remaining in the barracks stood as though at attention, pointing our ears toward the door. The voice of the other officer sounded familiar, but I couldn't quite place it.

The conversation quickly jumped several decibels as the two men continued barking at each other. As I eased closer to the door, I heard my name yelled out several times. I was hopeful that God would deliver me, but I was stunned at what I was hearing.

"You can't have Vanya!" my commander yelled. "He's off to the front tomorrow morning."

"You will immediately cancel his orders and place Vanya under my command," the other officer bellowed.

"Why are you insisting on taking Vanya?" my commander asked. "You could have any number of my soldiers who know how to make shoes."

"Vanya has skills I need, plus I want him to work for me."

How did this officer know of my cobbler skills, I mused. Who was he?

"You can't have him!" my commander shrieked again. "I will do everything in my power to keep him from you, and I will send him to the front. He disobeyed a direct order by refusing to take a weapon. I won't let this pass without disciplining him."

"How dare you speak to me like this!" the other officer yelled. "If you don't reassign him to my detail immediately, it'll be you heading to the front tomorrow!"

The two officers railed on each other for several more minutes; then one stormed off in anger. The next thing I knew the barracks door had flung open and an officer was shouting, "Vanya Yakovich, report!"

I saluted and said, "Vanya Yakovich Iliyn, sir!"

It was then that I noticed the officer's name tag: Beardin.

What I thought was just a chance meeting earlier in the day ended up being my salvation. Beardin was the commanding officer in charge of the factory that supplied boots to all the soldiers. He was short and portly and sported a distinctive handlebar mustache. His rank as a major gave him clout.

Major Beardin became my guardian angel, protecting me during my yearlong stint in the Russian army. He was an excellent cobbler, an expert when it came to using the sewing machine. But Major Beardin didn't know how to cut out the patterns and do the preparatory work. Since that was my expertise, he would come to rely quite heavily on my skills. My new commander was kind and protective of me. The other cobblers knew of my refusal to take up arms and did all they could to ridicule me. They all had to stand guard with their rifles, even though they were cobblers. Whenever I was commanded to stand guard, Major Beardin would intervene and cancel the order. Because of his protection, I never had to hold a rifle during my entire time in the army. Instead, I made boots.

The Turkestanskaya War ended in early 1946, but I remained in the army until the following spring. Soon after I was released, Major Beardin invited me to vacation with him at his cottage near Gulja. For the next three months, I lived with him and helped him harvest honey. Every day brought new discoveries for me as he taught me all about bees and honey. He loved his fifteen hives and knew how to make them produce the maximum amount of honey. I was fascinated with the work ethic of the bees, the dependence the bees had on their queen, and the incredible orderliness of the hive.

The day before I had planned to return to Uncle and Aunt's home in Gulja, my host pulled me aside for a long and serious talk.

"Vanya, did you enjoy your time here with me?" he asked.

"Very much so. You made me feel almost like a son, and I loved learning how to work with bees. I will never forget this time with you."

Beardin shifted nervously in his chair. "Vanya, I'm so glad you had a good time. I have been thinking, though, about the future. You're a wonderful cobbler, and I have plans to open a shoe store. With your skills, we could have the best store in Gulja. Stay with me, Vanya, and help me start this store. Please?"

Beardin had spoken to me about this idea on other occasions, but something was different about this time. He seemed to be begging me, leaning in close with a look of anguish on his face.

"I can't start the store without you," he implored. "You and I work so well together that I actually believe we were meant to be partners. Don't say no, Vanya. Think about the possibilities, about the future."

Beardin was so convincing that I almost said yes right then and there. But deep in my heart I knew God had something else for me. Uncle had already told me that God was directing us to leave Gulja for Shanghai and that we would be departing soon. And yet I didn't want to disappoint Beardin, who had been so kind to me these past eighteen months.

"I would really like to work with you if it would be possible," I answered. "But my destiny is not to stay here in China. God is leading us to Shanghai and then on from there. I hope you understand why I can't remain with you and help start this store."

Beardin's eyes glistened, and a tear slowly trickled down his cheek. "You have become like a son to me," he said. "I only want what's best for you. If this is what you have to do, then go and find your destiny."

I could no longer hold back my tears as he wrapped his large arms around me and hugged me long and hard.

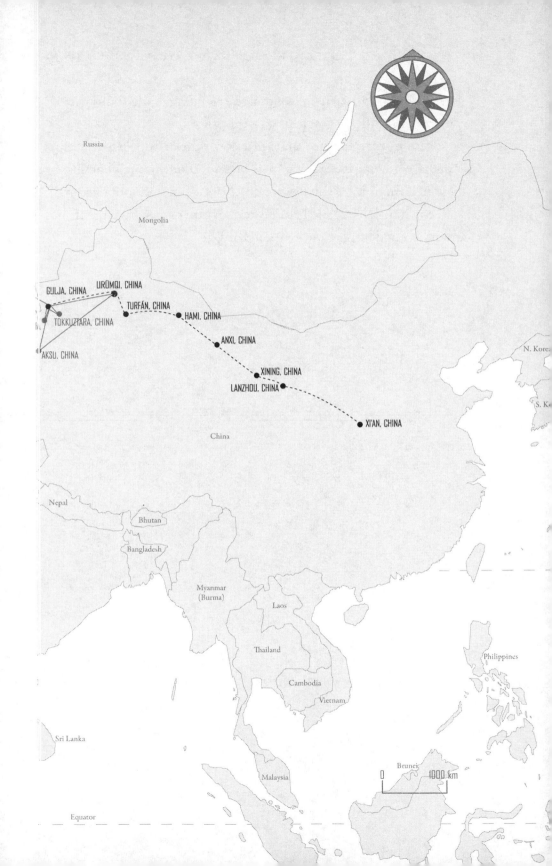

FOURTEEN

SHORTLY AFTER I had come home from the army, Lena walked back into my life. I was having dinner with Uncle and Aunt when our neighbors called us outside. I looked out the window. Joseph and Marusia were leading a girl up the dirt path toward our front door. I couldn't see the girl's face, but her walk looked familiar.

"Lena!" I shouted as I shoved my chair away from the table. Still clutching a warm tookach in my hands, I darted from the house as fast as my feet could carry me.

"Lena, is that really you?" Running past Joseph and Marusia, I fell into the arms of my sister.

"Vanyushka, Vanyushka!" Lena began to cry.

"I knew God would answer my prayer," I said, hugging Lena as tightly as I could and sobbing deeply.

"You prayed to see me again?" Lena said as she looked at me.

161

"Four years ago," I said, accidentally wiping my eyes with the tookach, "as our truck pulled away and I waved goodbye to you there in Urümqi, I prayed and asked God to please let me see you again." Lena looked puzzled as I continued. "And here you are. God answered my prayer."

"Vanya, God had nothing to do with this."

I was taken aback by Lena's reply, but before I could ask her what she meant, Uncle Mitrofan and Aunt Maria came up and were hugging my sister.

"How did you get here from Urümqi?" a bewildered Uncle Mitrofan asked.

"I used the money Misha left me, plus the medical school awarded me a sum of money based on my academic excellence," Lena said. "The school even encouraged me to spend the summer with my family."

"You're going to be with us for three months?" I exclaimed.

"Yes!" Lena gushed. "But I will have to get back to my nursing school by October."

Aunt Maria finally spoke. "Welcome home."

During the next several weeks, it became clear to me why Lena had answered me the way she did: she no longer believed in God. Uncle had many talks with her, only to be rebuffed by the atheistic training she had received both from the families she had lived with and from the schools she had attended. Every time I set off to our youth service, Lena refused to go. Instead, she went to dances with other non-Christian friends she had met in town. I was getting very worried for my sister and spent much time praying for her salvation.

Then one day Lena happened to be in the adjoining room as Uncle and Aunt led a prayer meeting in our living room. The prayer time lasted two hours, and at one point God spoke prophetically through Uncle Mitrofan: "Children, do not lose hope. For I will lead you far, far away, all the way to America. Just trust me."

That evening, Lena had a strange look on her face.

"What's the matter?" I asked.

"What will happen to me when you all leave for America?" she said.

Soon Lena became interested in prayer meetings and even our youth services. She began asking questions about God and how to pray. I often saw her speaking to Uncle about the Bible, and she even asked me questions about my faith. For one month, Lena attended all our youth services and even came to church on Sundays with us. I could tell something was happening in her life.

And then it happened! Lena came bounding home one day from youth service, ran into the kitchen, and yelled, "I'm saved, I'm saved!" Uncle Mitrofan and Aunt Maria embraced her and began crying tears of joy. I ran up and embraced the three of them. And there we stood in the middle of our living room—my family—weeping, hugging, and holding on to each other, .

The next month flew by. Uncle and Aunt were feverishly preparing to leave Gulja along with five other families. Uncle told me that the United Nations High Commission for Refugees (UNHCR) had agreed to help relocate us to another country. We would be the first Christian Russian group to receive this help. I marveled at how God used this newly formed organization to fulfill His prophetic words to us.

In mid-September of 1946, six families, a total of forty people, set out on a journey across China. Joseph told me that hopefully he and Marusia, along with their oldest two children, Nida and Peter, would catch up with us later, since they planned to leave in December. Misha and Nadya, along with their two sons, Victor and Walter, felt in prayer that the Lord was directing them to stay in China. Lena decided not to go back to school, but instead to go with us to America.

The UNHCR rented us a large flatbed truck, onto which we piled all our belongings. Twelve-foot-high boards were inserted vertically into slots along the sides of the flatbed. Ropes attached to these boards secured all our belongings. All the women and children sat in the middle of the truck atop our belongings. The men dangled their legs from the sides of the truck, hanging onto the vertical boards.

Our journey took us from Gulja to Urümqi and then on to Turfán. I was told it was good that we were traveling in September and not in July. Turfán was known as the hottest place in China, with typical summer temperatures climbing to 110 degrees. People said that from the ground, the reflected heat could measure up to 160 degrees. It was still hot in September, but I was grateful we were not traveling in July.

We spent the nights in caravanserais that dotted the dusty, pot-holed roads connecting each city. While in Turfán, we purchased bags of raisins and other dried fruit. From Turfán we traveled to Hami, Anxi, and Xining, and finally after three weeks we arrived in Lanzhou. The UNHCR put us up in a caravanserai on the outskirts of the city, where we lived for the next six months.

One day as I was making my way along the noisy, bike-strewn streets of Lanzhou, I spotted Paul Shevchuk from our group selling raisins. Chinese people were crowding all around him, shoving and pushing each other, trying to buy his raisins. I couldn't understand why he had attracted such a crowd. After all, there were dozens of raisin peddlers along the road, but none with a crowd like this. I approached Paul with curiosity when his supply ran out.

"What's happening here, Paul?" I asked. "Why are all these Chinese buying raisins from you?"

"It's strange, Vanya. I think they believe these raisins are from Russia because I'm Russian. Some of them said they'd never tasted Russian raisins. Before I knew what was happening, all my raisins were sold."

"We also have raisins we bought in Turfán!" I exclaimed as I ran back to the caravanserai.

For the next six months, we all made our livelihood by selling raisins. When we ran out of the raisins we had earlier purchased in Turfán, we bought more at the local wholesale fruit market. Because we were Russians, our raisins sold out almost instantly. The poor Chinese raisin peddlers scratched their heads in amazement. After all, our raisins were just like their raisins. We even expanded our inventory to include dried apricots and dried plums. No matter what we tried to sell, the Chinese bought. In six months, we had sold more raisins and other dried fruit than any other peddler in Lanzhou. Once again, God had provided for us in a most unusual way.

In April 1947 we set off for Shanghai. The UNHCR provided us with a Chinese host who spoke Russian. Our host accompanied us to the city of Xi'an where, he said, we would catch a train all the way to Shanghai.

When we arrived at Xi'an's overcrowded train station, our host purchased tickets and found a place for us to spend the night. Our train was to depart the next morning, and we had to carry all our belongings through the train station. I don't recall ever seeing so many people crammed into such a small building. It was like swimming in a sea of people.

As we settled in, I noticed several of our younger men speaking with two Chinese fellows. As I came closer, I could tell that the Chinese men were part Russian. They were curious about our group, asking questions about our destination and even asking to see our tickets. I found it interesting that they never left our side until our train arrived. They said that this was their train as well and that they would see us on board. But as soon as the train arrived in the station, we were separated in the surging sea of humanity moving toward the tracks.

Our men darted in and out of cracks in this wall of people, looking for space on the train for our group. From where I was standing, I could see Chinese people hanging out the windows, crowding around the stairs and doors of every train car. Still somehow more Chinese pressed their way onto the train. I did notice the two Russian-speaking men squeeze on board. As the train whistle signaled its warning to everyone of the train's imminent departure, still not one of our group had made it onto the train.

By now panic had set in. Our men started yelling at anyone willing to listen. They tried pushing their way onto the train but could not get inside. The train started moving, albeit slowly at first. The men yelled at us to grab our things and force our way onto the train. We tried hard to get on, but not one of us succeeded. As the train pulled away, we all gathered around our belongings, sweaty, haggard, and dejected.

"How could this happen?" someone said. "After all, God clearly wanted us on this train. We even had tickets purchased for us. What are we going to do now?"

People slumped onto their suitcases. We were all discouraged, and Uncle finally gathered us together and led us in prayer.

Right at that point, our Chinese host arrived with good news. He had explained our dilemma to the authorities, who told him of another Shanghai-bound train that would be arriving in two hours. Since it was a first-class train, we had to add a small amount of money for the new tickets, which we gladly did.

When the second train pulled into the station, it was practically empty, with nobody crowding to get on board. We walked on almost casually; no one pushed us or yelled at us. That first train had been a third-class train. How we thanked God as we boarded this nearly empty first-class train. Here we were, grumbling about not being able to get on a third-class train when all along God wanted to bless us with a first-class train. I heard many say, "Thank you, Jesus!" and

"Praise God," but I also heard others say, "O God, forgive us for not trusting You!"

As we approached one of the many stations that dotted the rail system, we noticed a large group of soldiers. When our train stopped, the soldiers boarded and asked who was in charge of our group. Our Chinese host came forward, and in my limited understanding of Mandarin, I could tell the soldiers were explaining to him that we would have to get off the train.

"But we have tickets all the way to Shanghai!" our host exclaimed.

"You will make it to Shanghai," a Chinese officer replied. "However, there's a situation we need to deal with before you proceed."

"And what could that be?" our host inquired.

The officer looked around at all of us. "The train ahead of you was also heading to Shanghai. It was stopped about forty kilometers outside this station by a band of revolutionary guerrillas who shot up the train and boarded it, apparently looking to kill a group of about forty Russians."

As he said this, he slowly glanced at each of us, almost as if he wanted to make sure we had heard exactly what he just said.

"Apparently their spies gave them some bad information, because they didn't find any Russians on board."

Our entire group let out an audible gasp. Immediately we all understood who those two Chinese-Russians were and why God had kept us off that train.

As we were contemplating what had just happened, the soldiers disconnected our engine and two train cars and sped off to fight the guerrillas. A couple of hours later we could hear sounds of a battle raging in the distance. We dropped to our knees and thanked our heavenly Father for protecting us in spite of our grumbling.

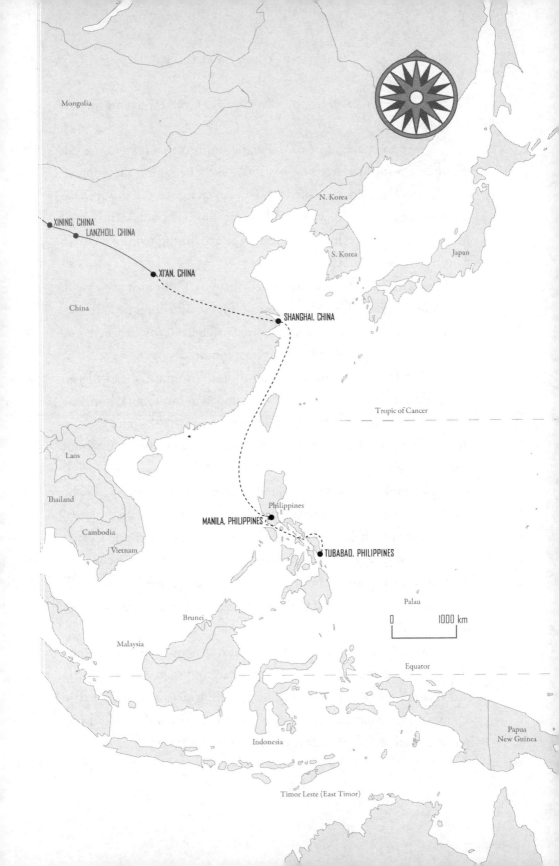

FIFTEEN

SPRING WAS IN full bloom when our train pulled into the Shanghai train station in May 1947. Large United Nations trucks quickly whisked us away to one of several cavernous old warehouses. Dust filled the air as our group of forty people, laden with all our belongings, shuffled along the dirt floor. Hundreds of metal beds covered with stained white sheets dotted the warehouse floor. Room dividers made of multicolored sheets hung from wires strung throughout the room. Each family was assigned a "room" based on the number of family members.

Our room was one of the smaller ones. Aunt Maria quickly pulled the sheets around our beds and began setting up our home. I noticed that the Zhernovys lived just a few thin sheets from us. Though I had often seen Lily during the past several years and even visited her home, I suddenly really noticed her. She was beautiful. Now, every time I saw her, I would get butterflies in my stomach. Plus my mouth would go dry whenever she spoke to me. What was happening to me?

Within a month, I was working two jobs: repairing shoes during the day and guarding a warehouse at night. Uncle Mitrofan helped with the distribution of UN food packages to our group and to other refugees who had recently arrived in Shanghai. Four months after arriving, we finally left the warehouse and moved into a tiny, run-down house that Uncle rented from a Chinese family. This was our home for the next year. In May of 1948, another large Russian group, which included the Shevchenkos, arrived from Gulja.

Uncle Mitrofan and the other men found a small Baptist Russian church that welcomed us with open arms. When Alex Shevchenko arrived from Gulja, he formed a choir, and soon, every Sunday, music filled that small Baptist church. For the next seven months, we sang and worshiped together with our new Russian Baptist friends.

I had never before had feelings for a girl like those I had for Lily. Since Misha was living in Gulja, I had no one I could speak to about these feelings. So I poured my heart out to God.

One day I decided to tell Lily about my feelings for her. As I approached her, my heart felt like it was in my mouth. I couldn't believe how much sweat could come out of my pores. My shirt was drenched, my knees were knocking, and my throat was dry. We sat on a bench outside our church building. I turned to Lily. "I really like you and want to ask you something important."

Lily looked at me with her big eyes and said, "I like you too."

With my hopes high, I continued. "We have been friends for several years, and I wanted to see if you would be willing to spend the rest of your life with me."

I hoped it was okay to say it that way. Lily just looked at me and smiled.

Taking that as an encouragement, I finally blurted out, "I would like to marry you."

Lily blushed and quickly looked at the ground. Then she glanced upward into my eyes and simply said, "That would be okay with me."

The next few months were blissful. We often saw each other at youth meetings, went on outings with the youth, sang together in the choir, and visited each other's home. Aunt Maria didn't even mind Lily and encouraged me to marry her. My heart was set on marrying her, and I even began thinking about the wedding. Then everything came to a crashing halt.

One day Paul Shevchuk approached me after one of our youth outings. Although I was acquainted with Paul, he was not one of my friends. Lily was with him when he said, "Vanya, I need to talk to you."

My stomach lurched and my heart skipped a beat.

"Okay," I muttered, looking at Lily.

"I see you like Lily. Actually, Lily and I have a serious friendship."

I was stunned to hear Paul's words.

"What do you mean, a serious friendship?" I asked.

"I want to marry her," Paul said.

"And does Lily agree?" I asked, looking expectantly at Lily.

Paul looked down at the ground. "Actually, she does."

"I need to hear it from Lily." My voice was shaky, and tears were pooling in my eyes.

"I'm sorry for this, Vanya, but it's true." Lily couldn't look me in the eyes but kept glancing at the ground as she spoke. "I know you asked me to marry you, but I'm going to marry Paul."

"Oh, well, I'm happy for you two." I didn't know what else to say. Paul shuffled his feet, folded his hands, and then turned and walked away. He looked back, beckoning Lily to follow him. I thought I detected a tear in Lily's eye as she awkwardly turned and ran toward Paul.

I was left standing alone, holding my bleeding heart in my hands, once again feeling abandoned and deeply hurt. Tears ran down my cheeks. I wanted to hide from people, to cry, to yell. Where were those dark corners when I needed them? I could almost feel the pain of Masha's beatings, but this time the pain was in my heart.

I ran aimlessly, looking for something, yet not knowing exactly for what. Then I saw it: a grove of apple trees. I dived onto the ground under the comforting cover of those trees. I sobbed deeply as I poured out my hurting heart to the only One who understood.

"Not again, Father!" I cried. "My heart feels like it's going to explode."

I slammed my fist into the soft earth beneath me. "Masha's pain was horrible, but I endured it, though at times I can still feel her blows on my back. But this . . . this pain I can't even explain. It's somewhere deep in my heart. I hurt in a way I've never hurt before. I thought she loved me. How could she . . . I could never . . . O God!"

I yelled and slammed both fists into the ground. I lay there sobbing, trying to understand my pain. I don't know how long I lay there, but I eventually fell asleep. It must have been in my dreams that I saw myself running into the outstretched arms of Jesus and feeling His strong embrace. Suddenly my pain just melted away.

When I awakened, the sun had gone down and it was getting dark. A light rain began to fall. I staggered to my feet, wiped my eyes and nose on my sleeve, and set out for home. I could still feel my pain, but I could also feel the strong arms of Jesus clutching me. Over the next few months, my pain began to slowly ebb. But would I ever again be willing to entrust my heart to another girl?

Shortly after arriving in Shanghai, I began to have stomach pains at odd times. At first the pain was barely noticeable, just a slight sting near my waistline right above my right hip. I thought maybe it was the unfamiliar food I was eating from the UN care packages. But then the pain became more acute, often forcing me to double over in intense discomfort. Because the pain was so erratic, I never mentioned it to Aunt Maria or to my sister Lena.

Uncle Mitrofan continued leading prayer meetings in our home. Even though we were uncomfortably crammed into our tiny house, we looked forward to these rich times of prayer and worship. God continued to speak to us. He said this was not the end of the journey. He was leading us on.

In January 1949 our group boarded the *Hwa-Lien*, a UN-sponsored refugee ship bound for the Philippines. We were the first wave of refugees being sent to the Philippines by the International Refugee Organization (IRO), an agency of the United Nations. After a brief stop in Manila, our two-week trip finally ended in Tubabao, a tiny island off the southern tip of Samar, six hundred kilometers southeast of Manila.

As we approached the island, I was amazed to see coconut palm trees everywhere along the shore. The first thing I did after we were processed by the authorities was to run up to a tall tree and stare straight up at the funny-shaped coconuts. As I stood there, wondering what they tasted like, someone poked me on my left arm. I was a bit startled by the lightly clad, dark-skinned Filipino boy standing next to me.

The boy smiled at me, and in his outstretched hand he was holding what looked like a shiny, white bowl with brown bark on the outside. The boy kept thrusting the thing at me, saying something in a strange language. I realized he wanted me to take it and eat it. I backed away, trying to politely refuse his gift. Suddenly he pointed up to the palm tree, then back to the white bowl in his hand. He smiled. It was then that I realized he was offering me, for the first time in my life, a taste of a coconut. As I took it from him, he ran off, skipping and laughing. I called my sister Lena over, and together, with our backs against a tall palm tree, we slowly ate the coconut, savoring each bite.

Before we could finish our coconut feast, Aunt Maria began shrieking at us. "Get over here immediately! What are you eating?"

"It's coconut," I said. "Would you like to taste some?"

She grabbed it out of my hand. "Where did you get this?" she demanded.

"A Filipino boy gave it to me."

Her hand went up, and anticipating her actions, I almost cried as I said, "Please, don't throw it away! It's really good and—"

"Silence!" she barked, as she hurled the piece of coconut toward the sea. "Now get in line. The authorities are taking us to the refugee camp."

Lena and I joined a throng of several hundred refugees, mainly Slavs, and grabbed our belongings in preparation to leave.

"Why is Aunt always so mean?" Lena fumed. "She didn't have to throw that piece of coconut away!"

"I'm sure she was just being extra careful for our sake. She didn't want us to get sick."

I could tell my answer didn't appease my sister's anger, and I quickly added, "Hey, don't worry about the lost coconut. I'll climb a palm tree and get you a fresh, big coconut all your own."

Lena finally smiled.

Thus began our eight-month stay in the Philippines. The refugee camp was located in a large, open field surrounded by jungle. The luggage of all five hundred refugees who disembarked the *Hwa-Lien* was dumped in a huge pile in a clearing next to the camp. Aunt Maria was furious when we told her about the luggage. Once we found our luggage, we were instructed to select a tent, clear a place in the jungle, erect our tent, and settle down. I had never before seen so many green army tents.

As we entered the camp, many tents were still lying on the grass, waiting to be assembled. The US Army stamp was clearly visible on all the tents. Some soldiers were erecting tents, while others were directing traffic. There were rows and rows of tents, some large enough to hold several hundred people, others small enough for a family of eight. I overheard some of our men speaking with the soldiers who told them the camp had beds for fifty-six hundred people.

The only furniture provided in each tent was military-style metal beds. These beds were peculiar in that each one was completely enclosed by a very fine netting. I had never seen such a net and asked why it was needed. A UN worker told me that as soon as the sun went down, I would find out.

And find out I did! That evening, hordes of blood-thirsty mosquitoes attacked us. So many of them were buzzing around our heads that it was impossible to stand still without frantically waving our hands. We ran for cover, searching for a safe haven without mosquitoes. That was when I realized why they had given us that fine netting that surrounded our beds.

Every night, our most important task was to make sure the mosquito netting was properly in place. If the net had even the smallest hole in it, sleep would be impossible. If anyone even leaned up against the netting, the mosquitoes would attack mercilessly. It was quite obvious each morning who had accidentally rolled up against the net.

Our family lived in a medium-sized tent shared with two other families. Military food rations were distributed daily. Crude outhouses were set up on the outskirts of our tent city, and most of us washed in the ocean. Since the water was so warm, we spent much time on the beach and in the water.

The camp officials quickly realized that many of us were Christians and offered us a large tent as a place to meet and worship. Close to 150 people were in our group alone. We joined with the Baptists and held joint services during our entire stay at the camp. A joint choir was organized, led by my brother-in-law, Joseph Lokteff. Joseph and Marusia had arrived at the camp several months before us. Joseph was a self-taught music teacher and a talented choir director. Soon visitors were streaming into our services to listen to the wonderful singing of our joint choir.

Our youth group was also flourishing. We quickly befriended the Baptist youth and formed one large united youth group along with a joint choir. Michael Lokteff, Joseph's older brother, became our youth leader. Michael's zeal for the Lord and his love of music had a profound impact on all of us. For the eight months we were at the camp, we worshiped and played together without the historical denominational differences of our past. God wove us into a tight family who truly looked out for one another. Our prayer meetings would often last three hours. Michael loved to pray, and his passion for God inspired us all.

When we began the youth group, I couldn't have imagined what a critical role it would play in my life.

ONE MONTH AFTER arriving in the Philippines, I was walking back to our tent with Lena when suddenly I doubled over in pain.

"Vanya! What's the matter with you?" she cried.

"My stomach hurts real bad."

"Can you walk?" she asked, crouching down next to me.

The pain was far more intense than I'd felt before, but I tried to be brave.

"I think so," I said as I struggled to stand.

As Lena grabbed my left arm to help me up, she touched my forehead. "Vanya!" she gasped. "You're burning up!"

Beads of sweat were dripping down my cheeks, and my shirt was suddenly drenched. I could barely stand, much less walk. The pain in my side was not subsiding as it always had before. It felt like someone was stabbing me in the side and twisting the knife. I slumped onto the ground and could hear my sister screaming for help. I felt arms picking me up. I was being carried by several men and heard them say to take me to the medical tent. The nurse in charge quickly checked me. "He is seriously ill," she said, "and we don't have the facility to help him. You're going to have to take him to the hospital."

By now the pain was unbearable. The pressure inside my body kept increasing, but I couldn't get any relief. I felt as though I would blow up.

"O God! Please help me!"

Uncle Mitrofan and Aunt Maria were now standing over me.

"What's the matter with Vanya?" Uncle asked.

"He is gravely ill," the nurse replied, "but we don't have a doctor who can help him. We must get him to the hospital in Guiuan."

I could hear Uncle speaking with several other men. Strong arms again lifted me up and carried me to a waiting military jeep. A soldier was sitting at the wheel, and Lena jumped in beside me.

"Please hurry!" she said to the driver, who sped off in a cloud of dust.

The ride to Guiuan took only forty-five minutes, but to me it felt like an eternity. The road was full of monstrous potholes, and I felt every single bump and dip. The pain was no longer just around my stomach but had spread throughout my body. I felt as though someone had blown me up with air and every access out was blocked.

"Open the windows!" I yelled. "I'm burning up!"

Lena placed a wet rag on my forehead. "Vanya, the jeep has no windows. It's completely open."

I could hear her crying out to God for help. I also tried to pray, but it was impossible to concentrate on anything except the pain.

After crossing a short bridge built by the US military, we finally arrived in Guiuan. The driver and Lena half dragged, half carried me into the hospital. A nurse directed them to a free bed. Through a fog of fever and pain, I could hear the moans of others around me. The hospital was one large room full of sick people lying on beds. I could see only one doctor attending all the patients. The doctor walked up to me, but instead of examining me, he knelt down by the bed next to me. I struggled to see what he was doing and noticed he was examining a very sickly looking man. The doctor began yelling instructions and then, just as suddenly, stopped. I saw him take the white sheet and extend it completely over the man's body, including his face. The doctor then turned and faced me.

"What's the matter with you?" he asked, touching my forehead.

Lena spoke for me through shakes and tears. "This is my brother, Vanya, and he's very sick. Something is wrong with his stomach."

The doctor pulled out his stethoscope and began a quick exam.

"Tell me where it hurts," he said as he tapped his fingers on my stomach.

He touched my right side and I screamed.

"Everything hurts!" I cried. "Doctor, I'm burning up! The pressure . . . it's . . . it's getting worse. I can't . . . help me get it out!"

"Oh no!" the doctor exclaimed. "His appendix has ruptured! Nurse! A bag of ice and penicillin. Now!"

Ice bags were piled on my face and chest. A nurse pulled back my sleeve and doused my arm with a cotton swab. I saw the needle as it sank into my arm. I expected instant relief, but none came.

The doctor beckoned to my sister, and I watched as they spoke. I could just make out the last part of his sentence as he said, "Who do you think I am? God? Your brother is as good as dead."

Lena covered her face with her hands and cried. She looked like she wanted to scream. The doctor placed his hand on her shoulder and said something else into her ear. He then pointed toward the back of the hospital room. I followed his gaze and saw a door.

Lena was still crying as she sat next to my bed. I could tell she wanted to say something to me but couldn't. Her eyes were so sad as she looked at me. I knew whatever the doctor had told her about my condition was not good. I also knew it because I felt like I was slowly dying.

"Lena," I whispered.

She leaned in so close I could feel her warm tears dripping onto my cheeks.

"I'm feeling worse. Everything hurts inside," I said as my speech began to slur. "Go back to the camp and tell them to pray for me. Tell Michael to have the youth pray for me. Everyone who believes in Jesus. Please, Lena. Pray."

Lena was crying as she placed new ice packs on my head. "I don't want to leave you like this, Vanya." She slowly stood and began nudging my bed in the direction the doctor had pointed.

"Where are you taking me?" I asked.

"The doctor wants you to have your own room."

As Lena bent down to kiss me, she threw her arms around my neck and sobbed uncontrollably. Then she stood up and hurried out the door. I wondered whether it would be the last time I would see her here on earth.

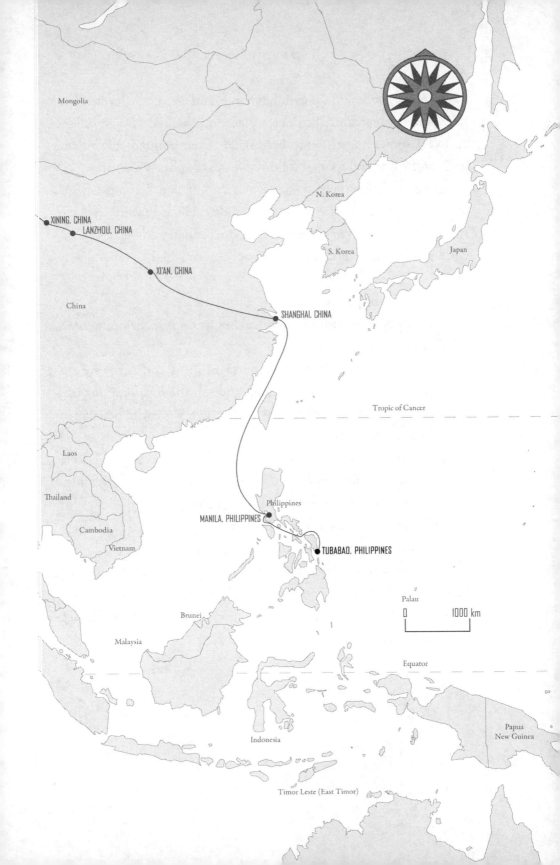

SIXTEEN

THROUGH BURSTS OF PAIN I tried to focus on the only visible object in my dingy little room—a rusty circular clock on the wall. It read 8:30 PM as Lena walked out. I felt so alone when she left the room. Thankfully, nurses came by regularly to check on me. They seemed upset that they weren't able to ease my pain. The doctor heard my screams and came by several times, instructing the nurses to give me more penicillin and to replace the melted ice packs on my face and body. But I could tell from their body language the shots and ice were having little effect.

During the 10:00 PM visit, a nurse placed a bedpan at my side. The pressure inside my body kept building. I could almost feel the poison spreading into my hands and my legs and down to my toes. I was dying. I knew it. Now all I could do was wait. It was just me, Jesus, and the pain. With what little breath I could muster, I whispered, "Papa. Mama. I'm coming home."

The room seemed to darken, a friendly darkness just like all those corners in Masha's house. I felt like I was six years old again, beaten by Masha for not finding enough eggs. I remembered that while I was on my knees in that dank, smelly barn, I would talk to Jesus. Only Jesus truly knew what I was going through.

"Jesus!" I prayed. "You understand. You know me. I'm really hurting this time. And it's not from Masha's strap. I think my appendix has ruptured, but You know what's causing this pain."

Every part of my body ached. The fever raged on, and my pillow was dripping wet, both from sweat and the melting ice packs. I couldn't sleep, and I seemed to be slipping in and out of consciousness. I soon realized that the nurses had stopped coming by to check on me. No more needles of penicillin. They probably decided it was a waste of medication. I remember the look on one nurse's face as she walked out and glanced back at me. Her eyes were sad. It was as if she was looking at me for the last time.

Then at three in the morning I felt it. I knew what time it was because the pain had twisted me so violently I found myself staring at the wall with the old clock. I had reached the breaking point. My teeth were clenched and my fists tight. Tears were running down my cheeks, mixing freely with the sweat that gushed from every pore.

Suddenly a bolt of electricity smashed into my head. It was so powerful that my head reverberated on the pillow. My eyes shot open, looking for the source. No one else was visibly in the room with me, but I knew it was Jesus. I had felt Him before.

The sensation careened down my neck and into my chest. It was as if someone was pushing everything inside me down, down toward my waist. The bolt surged through my chest, into my hands, and on into my stomach. I continued to shudder under its awesome power as it raced down each leg and into my toes.

The internal pressure became unbearable. I screamed.

"Nurse! Help me! I need . . . a toilet . . . please . . . help!"

I forced myself out of bed, grabbed the bedpan, and flung my frail body onto it. How it happened, I don't know, but all that poison, pus, and blood suddenly exploded out of my body and into the bedpan. The dam had burst.

I had a new body. At least that's how it felt. Jesus, my trusted Friend, had touched me and healed my broken body. I couldn't see Him, but I knew He was there. He felt so close, so real. I don't know how long I lay there, but it felt like clouds were holding me up. No pain, just sheer calm, like a feather floating peacefully with no care in the world. I wanted this feeling to last forever.

"Thank you, Jesus," I whispered.

At around 8:00 AM the door flung open and in walked the doctor. He approached my bedside and stared down at me. I'm sure he expected me to be dead. When I looked back at him and smiled, he seemed to be in shock. He just stood there for over three minutes, lower lip slightly quivering and eyes unblinking. Finally he spoke.

"Mr. Iliyn, how are you?" he whispered, sincerity written all over his face.

"I feel good. God healed me."

The doctor shook his head in amazement, then declared to the nurses, "This was not because of my help. This could only have been God!"

"Yes, Doctor. It was God."

A few hours later, Lena came bounding into my room. "Vanya, is it true what they say? Tell me it's so, Vanya!" She ran up to my bedside and bent over my face, her breath warm against my cheek. "It is so!" she gasped. "You look so, well, so peaceful. Thank you, Jesus!"

She grabbed me by my shoulders and started hugging me and weeping for joy.

"Sis, careful. You might break my neck."

"Forgive me, Vanya. I'm just so happy."

Lena eased my head back onto the pillow and sat down beside me.

"It's a miracle, Vanya! You're supposed to be dead." Lena's eyes grew really big as she continued. "The doctor pulled me aside last night and told me your appendix had ruptured and the poison had spread throughout your body. He said you were going to die and that no one could help you. He said that at twenty-one, you were already as good as dead."

Lena reached over and tenderly touched my cheek. "I didn't want to leave your side, Vanya. I wanted to be here all night. But you insisted I go back to the refugee camp and gather all the young people together for prayer. Vanya, you should have been there! It was an incredible sight. Hundreds of people—both young and old, Baptist and Pentecostal—gathered to pray for you. We prayed fervently, asking God to heal you."

Her eyes spilled out fresh tears.

"I was so afraid you would die. I didn't want to lose my family again."

Lena clung to me as though someone was trying to steal me away from her. In that moment I felt so secure, so loved. My best Friend, Jesus, had miraculously healed my dying body, and now I was in the embrace of family. Lena's cleansing tears seemed to wash away all those awful memories of Masha and my other hardships. All those dark corners, those places of refuge, faded away. I was happy again. It felt good to be alive. To be free of pain. And to have family.

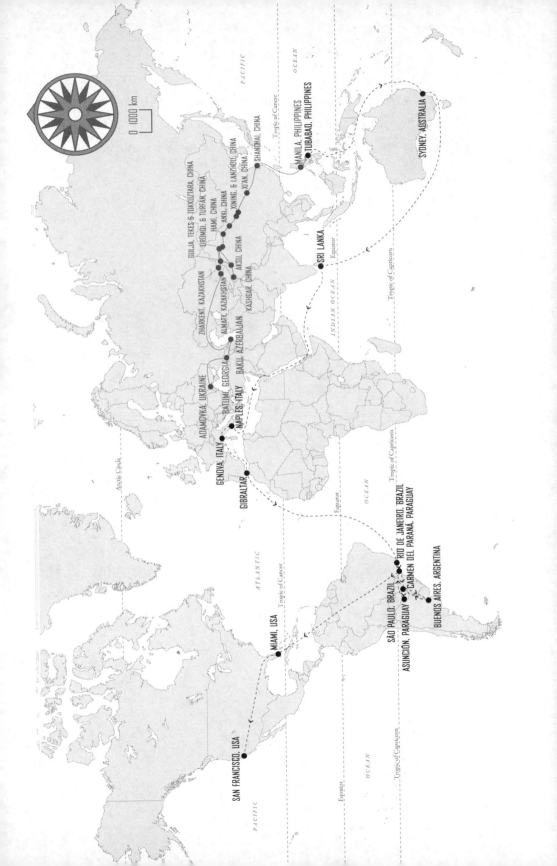

MANILA, PHILIPPINES
TUBABAO, PHILIPPINES
SHANGHAI, CHINA
SYDNEY, AUSTRALIA

GULJA, TEKES & TOKKUZTARA, CHINA
URUMQI & TURFAN, CHINA
HAMI, CHINA
ANXI, CHINA
XINING & LANZHOU, CHINA
XI'AN, CHINA

AKSU, CHINA

ZHARKENT, KAZAKHSTAN
ALMATY, KAZAKHSTAN
KASHGAR, CHINA

SRI LANKA

BAKU, AZERBAIJAN

ADAMOVKA, UKRAINE
BATUMI, GEORGIA
NAPLES, ITALY

GENOVA, ITALY

GIBRALTAR

RIO DE JANEIRO, BRAZIL
CARMEN DEL PARANA, PARAGUAY

SÃO PAULO, BRAZIL
ASUNCIÓN, PARAGUAY
BUENOS AIRES, ARGENTINA

MIAMI, USA

SAN FRANCISCO, USA

PACIFIC
OCEAN
Tropic of Cancer
Equator
INDIAN OCEAN
Tropic of Capricorn
Arctic Circle
Equator
OCEAN
Tropic of Capricorn
ATLANTIC
Tropic of Cancer
OCEAN
Equator
Tropic of Capricorn
PACIFIC
OCEAN

0   1000 km

O N SEPTEMBER 23, 1949—almost eight months to the day after we arrived in the Philippines—we boarded the USS *Marine Jumper* to begin a three-month voyage to Paraguay in South America. Our new "home" was an old, gray military transport ship, now packed with war refugees. Our party of over one hundred people included the Shevchenkos and other friends from the old country.

Alex Shevchenko told me his family had decided to come after a special Paraguayan land commission visited our camp in the Philippines. These commissioners were recruiting refugees willing to resettle in Paraguay and help farm the land in their underdeveloped country. They promised both land and farm equipment to help refugees establish their homesteads. Many of those in our party jumped at this opportunity for a new life in a new land. Some, however, decided to stay behind with hopes of being resettled in America. That included

Joseph and Marusia and their three children: Nida, Peter, and Reuben. Marusia was more than seven months pregnant, and our ship did not have medical facilities to accommodate her pregnancy.

"I know we will see one another again," Marusia said, gushing big tears. Lena and I wept with her, praying that God would allow us to reunite soon.

I recalled the prayer time we had had several months before we left, when God clearly spoke to us about a very long sea journey that lay ahead of us. God also said we would sing praises to Him on the high seas. We couldn't have imagined what a long and difficult journey it would be.

The first stop of our voyage was Sydney, Australia. From there we rounded Australia and spent fourteen days traversing the Indian Ocean, stopping only for a short port of call in Sri Lanka. I spent as much time as possible on deck, hoping to see whatever sights there were. The days at sea were mostly long and tedious, with few sightings of interest. That began to change as we entered the Gulf of Aden and traveled up the Red Sea toward the Suez Canal. Off to the east was the mysterious desert of Arabia, and to the west we could make out the coastline of Ethiopia and Egypt. These were places I had heard about from many Bible stories, and I was eager to see them.

The ship's captain permitted us to gather in a large stateroom for Sunday church services. We also practiced and sang as a choir, often for both the crew and the passengers. One Sunday morning as we were crossing the Suez Canal and our choir was singing, I again recalled the earlier prophecy. God had kept His word. We indeed were praising Him on the high seas.

Shortly after clearing the Suez Canal, we were engulfed in a terrifying storm. I had never seen such a violent upheaval, much less been in the middle of one. Waves rose and crashed onto the deck, tossing our ship around like a toy boat in a bathtub. Many passengers were paralyzed with fear, and crewmen moaned about a Mediterranean ship graveyard.

Most of the crewmen ran out on deck trying desperately to secure the ship's hatches and keep the vessel afloat. The passengers were instructed to go below and gather near the center of the ship. The crew handed out bags to all of us, which at first puzzled me. But as the storm intensified, the purpose for the bags became painfully obvious. Within minutes, the rolling motion of the ship had made everyone seasick. I began vomiting uncontrollably. Within the first twenty minutes, my bag was full and the stench on the ship was horrible.

As the storm pummeled our ship, I felt so bad I wanted to die. Others around me, covered with their own vomit, moaned in pain. I collapsed on the floor and cried out to Jesus. "Please, please help us. I . . . I trust You . . . I need You now."

"Vanya, come here!"

I looked up weakly and saw a blurry rolling image of Lena sliding up next to me. "They gave me some pills that are supposed to help with this seasickness," she said, thrusting a small pill into my hand. "Take this now!"

I was so sick I would have taken anything as long as it would take away this horrible feeling. I swallowed the pill, expecting instant results. Nothing happened. I just got sleepy, real sleepy.

Apparently I slept through the worst of the storm, because when I awoke, the ship seemed to be standing still. If it weren't for the awful stench, the storm would have seemed like just a terrible nightmare.

WE SAILED PAST the island of Crete, around Sicily, and stopped at Naples, Italy. We had been at sea for over five weeks. As we disembarked, I wanted to kiss the ground. During our one-month stay in a large transit camp full of refugees, we were allowed to visit many historical sites in Italy, including Pompeii and Rome. On our train ride up to Rome, Lena and I sat glued to the window, staring in awe at the beautiful Italian countryside. Everywhere we looked, we saw vineyards laden with huge, juicy grapes. The Italian countryside seemed so orderly, and the people were all so good-looking. Compared to where we had come from, this seemed like paradise.

Rome was like another world. The Colosseum and the Vatican dwarfed any buildings we had ever seen. As we wandered through St. Peter's Basilica and the Sistine Chapel, we were stunned at the sight of so many art treasures. Even ordinary streets had statues and buildings dating to early Greek and Roman times.

Soon we were back on a train headed toward Genova, where our group boarded a French ship bound for Marseille, Gibraltar, and then across the Atlantic Ocean to Brazil. In late November, after two more weeks at sea, we finally reached Rio de Janeiro. From there we took a train to São Paulo, where we boarded an old airliner for the final leg of our journey to Paraguay.

As we started our final descent for landing, I looked outside the window and didn't even see a paved road, much less a city or an airport. Alex Shevchenko was sitting ahead of me, and I leaned forward and asked, "Where are we going to land?"

Alex didn't seem concerned. "We're going to Carmen del Paraná, a tiny village in southern Paraguay, so it's probably just a small landing strip."

As the plane descended past one thousand feet, Alex craned his neck looking for the landing area. Then suddenly he shouted, "Brace yourselves! We're landing in a field!"

Sure enough, our plane touched down, rather roughly, right in the middle of a dirt field. Our grueling three-month trip had come to an end on December 19, 1949.

AS WE EXITED the plane, the first thing that struck me was the humidity and heat. I couldn't understand, since this was December. Why was it so hot? Alex explained that we were now in the southern hemisphere, where the seasons are reversed. December was the start of summer in South America.

A joyful crowd of believers came out to welcome us. I heard some of the locals tell Uncle Mitrofan they were taking us to a place called Operra in the Colony of Fram. This final leg of our journey made us wonder whether we'd made a mistake in coming here. The countryside was bleak, the weather was miserably hot, and the road was bumpy and dusty. The old bus creaked along, trying to avoid potholes big enough to swallow us up.

If that wasn't bad enough, no officials were waiting to greet us. That meant no free land, no tools, and no supplies to help us get started. Actually, not one of the promises those commissioners made to us was ever fulfilled. We were left on our own to tame this new land. If it hadn't been for the meager help we received from the local believers, we would have been left to starve.

During our first two weeks in Operra, we lived in old military dorms with dirt floors. Many nights we cried and wondered what we were going to do in this desolate place. Once we realized no help was coming from the Paraguayan government, we turned to God in prayer. More than once, God assured us that this was a temporary stop on our way to America. As soon as we had that hope, we applied ourselves to the task of living and working.

Uncle Mitrofan and his friend Keroosha had enough money saved to purchase a small farm. Most of the others had to carve their farms out of the wilderness. After working the farm for close to a year, Uncle Mitrofan and I realized we were not farmers. We sold our share to Keroosha and, with what little money we had saved up, began a shoe business in Carmen del Paraná.

Now I was doing what I loved. We rented a cramped little shop just off the town's main street. I purchased blocks of hard wood that both Uncle and I laboriously carved into different sized men's, women's, and children's shoe lasts. The lasts were rather crude but worked just fine. I then found some cheap leather and purchased enough to make several pairs of shoes.

What excitement I felt as the first customer walked into our dusty little shop and ordered the first pair of shoes. Uncle immediately started making the soles while I prepared the upper part of the shoes. These definitely were handmade shoes. It was with much pride that I took the money for that first pair.

Once the orders began building up and we had saved some money, I took a train to Asunción, the capital of Paraguay, and purchased professional maple shoe lasts. I also found an excellent source for leather and was able to buy an industrial sewing machine. With our meager earnings we rented a small storefront on the main street of Carmen del Paraná. On November 14, 1950, one day before my twenty-second birthday, we opened the doors of our new shoe store.

Though life was difficult in Paraguay, our church and choir helped us cope with our many hardships. Almost immediately after arriving in Paraguay, Alex organized both a youth choir and an adult choir. I sang bass in the youth choir. Besides singing at every Sunday morning and evening service, we were invited to every wedding that year. And there were many weddings!

I think it was at one of these early weddings that I first noticed a young woman so gorgeous I couldn't stop looking at her. Her eyes were stunning; they were haunting, mesmerizing me every time I looked at her. Her name was Sofia Neciuk. She was eighteen years old, and all the single guys in Paraguay wanted to marry her. I did, too, but what chance did I have? Would she even notice skinny Vanya, the orphan? Oftentimes I found myself staring at her in church, wondering what she was thinking. Should I even consider prying open my heart again, especially since my pain from Lily's rejection had just recently healed? Should I risk being rejected again?

Something compelled me to try. Somehow I knew that this time things would be different. Every evening as I knelt to pray, Sofia would invariably dominate my thoughts. My heart was slowly being pried open with an assurance from God that it would not be squashed this time.

It wasn't that my faith in God had ever wavered. He had never let me down or hurt me. But ever since Papa and Mama died, it was people, both well-intentioned and even Christians, who caused all of my pain and misery. I tried hard not to lose faith in people, but dark corners provided me more companionship and comfort. And yet something about Sofia made me willing once again to trust.

I remember well that evening when I allowed God to pry open my scarred, beaten down, and severely pained heart.

"You know how much I trust You," I cried. "You've been my papa and mama for the past seventeen years. When no one cared, You were always there, caressing me as I pressed myself deep into those dark corners, trying to escape the pain."

I winced as memories of Masha, flailing my back with her special leather strap, flashed before my eyes.

"Every time I was misunderstood and kicked out of my house, it was into Your open, comforting arms I ran. When I was left to die, You never left my side." I placed my hands on my heart and sobbed. "When people stepped on my heart, You picked it up and, with Your tears of understanding, gave it back to me, healed. I know I can always trust You. But can I trust another girl with my heart?"

My pillow became wet with tears as I plopped into bed, but my heart was no longer heavy. I felt an assurance deep in my spirit that things were going to work out differently this time. As I slowly drifted off to sleep, I could hear myself repeating over and over again, "I trust You. Here's my heart. I think I like Sofia . . ."

Sofia's parents owned a general store just down the street from our shoe shop. I found myself making any excuse I could think of to go to the store in hopes that I would see Sofia. She was the oldest in the family, and I quickly got to know two of her brothers, Bill and George. Her parents loved to sing, as did Sofia. Since I, too, liked to sing, this opened the door for me to visit their home. I spent many evenings at Sofia's home, talking to her parents and singing songs with Sofia and her parents.

Some evenings I would spend hours just sitting at the kitchen table, talking to Michael, Sofia's dad. In many ways, Michael reminded me of Papa. He was a kind, gentle man with a strong love for God. I loved to watch him interact with Nastia, his wife. Their love for each other was obvious. Michael was always helping Nastia around the house, even during my visits.

Nastia—short for Anastasia—was a great cook. Though I came to their home mainly to see Sofia, I also looked forward to Nastia's delicious home-cooked meals. During the next two months, I spent many of my free nights at Sofia's home, sitting at the table, eating, singing, and talking to her family.

Sofia and I took many walks together, talking, laughing, and just being together. One of our favorite things to do was walk to the train station and watch the steam engine train come chugging into the station.

As much as I wanted to see Sofia, I loved being with her parents. I had a longing in my heart for something they had. Many times I would find myself just watching them interacting with each other and their children. It was wonderful. *Maybe that's what a real family is like,* I thought. *Had Papa and Mama lived, they would have been just like Michael and Nastia.*

One day as I was sewing a pair of men's sandals, my mind suddenly wandered back to China, back to when I was four and a half years old. There I was, once again, slumped against the wall of the ditch by the road looking at mud oozing out of my dirty shoes and thinking about Papa. But this time I found myself saying, "I want to be just like Michael." That was the day I realized God had healed my heart.

I found myself thinking more and more about Sofia. As I prayed for her, I could feel emotions being stirred deep within my heart. Emotions that I thought had been buried for good were once again blossoming from within. It was almost as if layers of thick skin were being peeled back from my heart and love was being breathed back into my life. Sofia made me feel special, and her parents accepted me for who I was. To them, I was not an uneducated, skinny orphan; I was Vanya Iliyn!

As I knelt to pray one evening, my heart was overwhelmed with hope and love as I prayed. "Sofia is the one I want to spend the rest of my life with."

My friendship with Sofia was two months old when I realized I loved her and wanted to marry her. During these two months, I had been very careful not to violate my friendship with Sofia. Though I wanted to hold her hand and maybe even kiss her, I never succumbed to my feelings. Most of our time together was spent either in the presence of her parents or with other youth from church.

On December 15, Uncle Mitrofan and I visited Sofia's home with the intention of asking her parents for her hand in marriage. Though I was nervous, I felt an unexplainable peace in my heart. I somehow knew it would be okay. When Michael said yes, we all knelt and prayed. I couldn't hold back my tears as I poured out my gratefulness to God. My heart exploded with joy just thinking of Sofia, of my future family, of my future home. My home, my family, a real family—finally!

Our wedding took place on January 14, 1951, in our small church in Carmen del Paraná, Paraguay. The wedding was simple but beautiful. Sofia looked stunning in her pearly white wedding dress as she walked down the aisle alongside her father. Michael placed her hand into mine, and I shuddered with excitement as I curled my fingers tightly around her soft hand. The wedding was performed by our pastor, Anisim Koval. Most of the ceremony was a blur, although I will never forget raising Sofia's veil and kissing her soft lips for the very first time. I wanted that moment to last forever.

Before I knew what was happening, we were standing outside greeting all the well-wishers. As people hugged and kissed us, my spirit was elsewhere. I could see the people and even responded to their congratulations, but my mind was teeming with thoughts of gratefulness to God.

This is not a dream. I am really, really married. And look at my Sofia, my dove. So elegant, so gorgeous. I knew You wouldn't let me down, but this is more than I ever expected. She's so beautiful. And she's my wife. And God, I won't let You down. I will love her the way Papa loved Mama, the way Michael loves Nastia, the way You love me.

Our first eight months of marriage were blissful, filled with love and wonder. The day of our wedding, we moved in with Uncle Mitrofan and Aunt Maria. I continued working at our shoe store, while Sofia worked at her parents' store. Sofia, my little dove, brought such serenity and delight into my life. Though our days were often hectic and frenetic, our evenings were peaceful, idyllic. With the dark corners of my past behind me, the future looked rosy and promising.

By the second month of our marriage, Sofia was pregnant. Despite asking for strange foods at the most inopportune times and showing a bit more fatigue than usual, Sofia continued to work normally throughout her pregnancy. In early July, I was offered a better job working in an established shoe store in Buenos Aires, Argentina. Within days, we were on our way to Argentina.

For the next two months, I worked at the shoe store in downtown Buenos Aires, while Sofia remained at home. September 13, 1951, started like any other day. Spring was in the air. Our shoe store was unusually busy that afternoon as I answered an urgent phone call from home.

"Vanya, come home quickly!"

I could tell that Anna, our neighbor and close friend, was on the verge of hysteria as she screamed through the phone.

"Why?" I demanded. "What's wrong? Is Sofia okay?"

"She's really, really sick! I . . . I think she's going to . . ."

"Anna!" I yelled. "Tell me exactly what's wrong with Sofia."

"She's sweating profusely, and she's screaming. She's grabbing her stomach and—oh my!"

"Anna, what—"

"Her water just broke!" Anna shrieked. "Vanya, Sofia is giving birth!"

"What!" I screamed. "That can't be!" I was stunned. I stared at the phone and yelled even louder, "That can't be! Sofia is only eight months pregnant."

I gripped the phone so hard my knuckles turned white. I was so shocked I couldn't move. I felt riveted to the floor. My heart sounded like a snare drum, and my head began to swim. I could hear Anna yelling something but couldn't even bring the phone to my ear. I just stared at the phone in utter disbelief.

"This can't be happening," I mumbled. "What will people say?"

"I see the head!" Anna's hysterical voice sounded tinny, surreal. "Vanya!" I heard Anna yell. "I think it's a—"

I dropped the phone and bolted out of the room. I can't even remember exactly how I got home, but as I rushed inside, I could hear a baby crying. As I ran past a wide-eyed, giddy Anna, I faintly heard her say, "It's a girl, Vanya! You're a papa!"

I brushed past the women hovering around Sofia and suddenly found myself face-to-face with a baby, a girl, my daughter. I don't know how long I stood there, staring in utter amazement and disbelief.

"Vanya!" Sofia's crackling voice brought me back to reality. "What's the matter with you? You look like you're about to faint."

I realized my mouth was open, and I was beginning to sway from side to side. I felt dizzy, disoriented, excited, shocked. A sense of dread engulfed me like a storm cloud heavy with rain.

"Sofia," I muttered. "What happened? How could this . . . ? Um, she's so beautiful, uh, looks just like you. But it's been only eight months. What will people say? O God, what are we going to do?"

"Take her, Vanya. Hold your daughter." Sofia's soft voice instantly calmed my ruffled spirit as I bent down and gently picked up my first child, my daughter. Tears began coursing down my cheeks as I peered into her dark brown eyes. Wave after wave of emotion washed over me as I shuffled over to a chair and plopped down, clutching my daughter tightly against my chest. I didn't understand what was happening to me. On the one hand, I was overwhelmed with joy. *This is MY daughter! I'm a papa!* On the other hand, it was as if a black, ominous cloud of dread loomed just overhead, ready to swallow me up.

Only eight months, I thought. *How could she have been born after just eight months?* I was sure people in the church were going to question my integrity, my honesty. Was it actually possible for a baby to be born after just eight months? And yet, here I was, holding my daughter. I knew exactly what Sofia and I had done leading up to our wedding, so my conscience was clear.

And yet it was as if a powerful magnet was drawing me back toward my old friends, those dark corners. I knew I would be safe if only I could squeeze myself into a dark corner. Nobody would misunderstand me; no one would question my actions or my motives.

My daughter yelped and curled her hand around my index finger. It startled me. Her brown eyes stared at me so intensely I had to look away. My gaze drifted to her tiny hand grasping my finger. It was then that I heard God speak deep into my soul: "Faith, Vanya. Just have faith."

Instantly I knew my daughter's name would be Vera, meaning faith in Russian. As our little girl tenaciously clung to my finger, a smile appeared on my face.

How I love you, Vera, I thought. *I will always be here for you. You can trust me. I love you so much I'm willing to die for you!*

SHORTLY AFTER Vera's birth, I was called before the elders of our church and grilled for hours. Several of the men insisted I openly confess my sin. I told them I would be happy to do so, but there was no sin involved. Actually, if I were to confess some sin, I told them, I would be lying. I hadn't done anything wrong.

One of the men from our church continued to hound me every time he saw me. It became so severe that I avoided contact with him. On my knees, I poured out my frustrations and hurts to the only One who understood me, and my faith in God became stronger by the day. I realized that I didn't need to defend myself. The future would prove it so. It took several more years before all suspicion was gone.

Shortly after Vera was born, we received a letter from my sister Marusia and her husband, Joseph, who were now living in San Francisco, California. They had been able to immigrate directly to America from the Philippines shortly after we left for Paraguay, and had been living in San Francisco since December 1950. Marusia wrote me often, encouraging me not to give up my hopes and dreams of immigrating to America.

While still in the Philippines, I had filled out the appropriate paperwork to immigrate to America but was told that the normal wait time was three to four years. Joseph and Marusia had been faithfully searching for a guarantor for us since they had arrived in San Francisco and assured me in this letter that one had finally been found.

In preparation for our immigration to America, we moved back to Carmen del Paraná. Mitrofan welcomed me back to the shoe store. Business was brisk, and I began saving every penny I made for the upcoming trip. On February 13, 1954, Sofia gave birth to our first son, Peter. Shortly after this joyous occasion, we moved, along with Mitrofan and Maria, to Asunción so that we could be nearer to the

US consulate. Mitrofan and I opened a shoe store and once again saw our business prosper.

The US consulate was slow in providing answers to us about our visa, so I pushed ahead with the shoe store. My priority was to save as much money as I could, even though I knew I could never save enough to pay for our travel to America. But my faith in God and His promise never wavered.

Shortly after the birth of Peter, I began noticing a proliferation of jewelry stores throughout Asunción that specialized in selling gold coins from many different countries. Though I had several thousand dollars saved up, I knew it was not enough for the tickets, much less for any living expenses we would incur while in America. Sofia and I were praying one day, and both felt strongly from the Lord that we were to buy gold coins. I purchased gold coins from Mexico, Chile, and Russia, plus currency from America.

Our second son, Johnny, was born on November 15, 1955, and shortly after that, all sale of gold in any form came to an abrupt halt. The price of gold skyrocketed. Before I knew it, my gold coins were worth three times what I had paid for them. Not only did I have enough money for our tickets, but also we would have money left over once we arrived in America.

When that final letter arrived from the US consulate informing us of our approval for entry into the United States, Sofia and I knelt beside our bed and wept in gratitude before God. "You kept Your promise!"

Our preparation to leave was a whirlwind of activity. After selling our shoe business to a friend, we began packing all our meager belongings into our old suitcases. Mitrofan and Maria would be traveling to America with us. Our departure day had arrived: September 13, 1956. My sister Lena, her husband Anatoly, and their three sons,

John, Peter, and Tony, traveled to the airport with us. Lena wrapped her arms around me as she bade me farewell.

"Vanyushka, your journey is almost complete!" Lena exclaimed as she hugged me ever so tightly. "A new land awaits you. I will pray that God gives you a good and prosperous life. But don't forget your family."

"I won't." I hugged Lena even tighter. "I know we will be together soon in America."

"Don't forget Misha and his family in China," Lena continued. "He has four children now and is trying to immigrate to America as well."

Though I was leaving with my little family, I knew that God's promise to our parents would not be complete until my siblings and I were all together in America.

Our initial flight took us to São Paulo, Brazil. From there we boarded a plane for Miami, Florida. As the plane approached the Miami airport, I couldn't help but notice the incredible difference in terrain to that bumpy, overgrown field in Paraguay that served as our first landing strip. We touched down September 14, 1956. I barely remember the process of clearing customs and getting our luggage. The first thing I did once we stood outside the airport was to kneel and kiss the ground. America, my new home.

A four-day Greyhound bus ride to San Francisco awaited us. Joseph and Marusia met us there and welcomed us to their home. After our reunion, I stepped outside their house, needing a few minutes to myself.

"America!" I could barely speak as tears rolled down my cheeks. "You promised Papa and Mama that their family would one day be in a new land. Today, half of our family is here. I trust You to bring Misha and Lena here as well."

As I looked out over the skyline of San Francisco, I collapsed onto my knees, raised my hands skyward, and exclaimed, "Thank you, dear Father! You never did forget this little orphan boy. My heart is about to explode with gratitude for all You have done in my life. I will never forget it! The pain of my childhood is all but forgotten. I leave behind all my dark corners and I'm ready to embrace all You have for me and my family in this new land."

As I stood up, the door to the house flew open, and out ran Vera and Peter screaming excitedly, "Daddy, Daddy, we're in America! We like America!"

As they leapt into my arms, I kissed them repeatedly and hugged them tightly. Sofia came out with little Johnny, and we all stood together in the yard, clinging to each other, laughing, and crying. As I watched my wife and children, I made a promise to God in my heart. *They will hear of all the miracles You have done in my life.*

Sure enough, as we finally got settled into our first apartment on Geary Street, some of my most enjoyable moments were the storytelling times with my children as I prayed with them before bedtime. Vera and Peter would always beg me to tell them about my childhood.

"Children," I would begin, "when I was four years old, we were escaping from Russia to China. My mama was lost, and my papa was somewhere out in a rice field. I still remember like yesterday the first words out of my mouth, 'Papa, where are you?'"

AFTERWORD

AT THIS WRITING my father is eighty-two years old, living in retirement in Woodburn, Oregon, along with Sofia, the love of his life. Joseph and Marusia immigrated to America during the winter of 1950. Misha (Michael) and Nadya and their family immigrated to Australia in 1958 and to America in the spring of 1963. Anatoly and Lena Kozaczuk and their family immigrated to America in the winter of 1963. Marusia died in a car accident in July of 1978.

I decided to write this book because I wanted to honor my father, honor God, and give my children a written testimonial of their grandfather's life. I wanted them to know how a neglected orphan boy, deeply hurt and abused by those closest to him, never succumbed to bitterness but instead grew up with a profound sense of gratitude to God. I also hope that my father's life story will have a positive impact on the lives of many hurting people today.

We were extremely poor those first few years after arriving in America from Paraguay. Because none of us could speak English, Dad and Mom were forced to find any type of factory-assembly work. Mitrofan and Maria took care of us children.

We didn't own much in those days. Never had a television set. Our parents, however, always made sure we had good housing and lots of food. Life revolved around the table. Two more sisters, Lily and Rita, and a brother, Paul, were born in America.

We grew up speaking the Russian language mainly because our parents spoke no English. We also attended a Russian language school that our church in San Francisco organized. Three hours every Saturday for nine years we studied Russian grammar and literature. None of us kids liked the Russian school, but our parents would almost daily say to us, "One day you will be grateful we insisted you keep your Russian language. God will open doors for you to use your language."

For entertainment I read every Hardy Boys book I could find. But my favorite stories were those Dad would tell us at bedtime. Every evening, he would collect all the children on a warm down comforter my mother had made. Before Dad prayed for us, he would tell us a short story. These were not just any old stories; they were true stories about his childhood—snippets from his life, adventures in Russia, China, and South America. Every time Dad would end a story, we would shout, "Tell us another story, Daddy. Please!"

He would always say, "Tomorrow." And so we couldn't wait for Daddy to come home from work.

This book you just read includes the stories I grew up hearing year after year after year until they became part of my DNA. My father's life story has had a profound impact on my life. I like to say 90–95 percent of who I am and what I teach I gleaned from my dad.

I remember one of the first times my dad told us about Masha and the eggs. At the telling of the story, my dad thought Masha was still alive and living in Australia. We later found out she had died in China. As Dad told us about being beaten for not finding enough eggs, all of us kids piped up in unison, "That's not right, Daddy. Why did Masha beat you? It wasn't your fault you couldn't find those eggs. And why did she hate you just because you were a boy? That wasn't your fault either. Tell us where Masha lives, Daddy, and we will blow her house up and beat her up!"

All my dad had to do was to say, "That's right, children. Masha was a horrible woman and I hated her," and we would have all grown up with bitterness toward a woman we had never met. Instead, with tears in his eyes, Dad would always add, "Kids, don't hate Masha. If I were to meet her today, I would be the first person to run up to her, hug her, and thank her, because even though she hated me, at least she was willing to take care of a little orphan boy." Instead of planting seeds of bitterness into our tender, virgin hearts, my dad planted seeds of gratitude.

As I listened to how God became a Father to my dad, I remember thinking, *I like God because He took care of my daddy.* And so I fell in love with God. Secondly, I fell in love with my dad. I never did fall into any major sin as a boy, mainly because I loved my dad and I didn't want to bring any more pain into his life. After hearing about his life, I realized he had suffered enough.

Today, as an adult, I realize that this is the type of relationship God wants us to have with Him. He doesn't want us to serve Him because we are afraid of hell or because we want to go to heaven. He wants us to serve Him because we know Him and don't want to bring any more pain to His heart. My dad taught me the importance of having an intimate, personal relationship with God.

Shortly after arriving in America, Dad met two brothers who had recently opened a shoe store. Dad became the third partner in this venture. From then on, every free minute we had was spent in the shoe store. From sweeping floors to polishing shoes to delivering advertising, we stayed busy right through our childhood. The shoe store did well right up until 1968. During the next four years, business took a downturn, so much so that by 1972 the store had gone out of business.

Dad had to find another means of supporting the family. After spending his life working with shoes, he became a painter. The first six months of painting houses in San Francisco stressed his muscles so that he could barely move. But he didn't complain and didn't give up. Eventually he became an excellent painter.

About the same time, I was graduating from high school and on my way to university. My father had never had a chance to get an education, but he strongly encouraged us kids to pursue higher education. So you can only imagine how proud he was as he watched me flip my tassel. I had just received my bachelor of science degree in Electrical and Material Science Engineering from the University of California, Berkeley. It was June 1976, and all of my peers were getting excellent jobs in Silicon Valley. But I had so fallen in love with God that I wanted to serve Him as a missionary for the rest of my life.

Shortly after graduation, I sat down with my dad and discussed my future plans with him. "Dad," I said, "I love God and want to be a full-time missionary serving with Youth With A Mission in Los Angeles."

"That's wonderful, my son. I'm proud of you. And what will your starting salary be?" Dad asked.

"I won't receive one. I have to raise my own support, Dad," I mumbled.

My dad did not understand.

In the fall of 1976, I joined the staff of YWAM, Los Angeles. During the next eighteen months, I periodically came back home after traveling to various countries. Invariably my dad and I would have a conversation similar to the previous one. I was not rebelling against my dad as I continued to serve with YWAM. The mission teaches us to trust God for our financial needs. I was simply obeying God while praying and hoping for my dad's blessing.

A year and a half later when I came home again from the mission field, my dad and I had another conversation. But this time Dad said, "Son, I don't know why I do not have a peace about this. Let's pray about it."

I will never forget that prayer meeting. My dad, my mom, and I prayed for over half an hour. I watched my dad fall on his knees, raise his voice to God, and cry out, "Father, why don't I have a peace about what my son is doing? Please speak to me. I will not get up from my knees until I hear You speak to me."

Tears streamed down my father's cheeks, pooling at his knees as he cried out to God for an answer. When he finally got up, he fixed his eyes on me and said with authority, "Son, I know why I have not had a peace about this. God has clearly shown me the problem. He told me I was not willing to release you. Son, I now bless you and release you to pursue the very call God has placed on your life."

I felt like a canary inside a cage. It was as if my dad suddenly thrust the cage door open and exclaimed, "Son, fly!" Today that little canary has become an eagle.

As I look back on that incident, I realize that the reason my dad had a problem with my decision to become a missionary was his fear that without a salary I would be poor, just like he had been. When he agreed with God to release me, in essence what he was saying to God was, *God, here is my son. I entrust him into Your care and totally trust You to take care of him.* I have been humbled by God and His care during these past thirty-three years of full-time missionary work.

In the fall of 1978 I moved to Salem, Oregon, and joined the YWAM staff at the newly opened ministry center. It was here that I met a most beautiful and remarkable woman, Luba Svetlichny. Our engagement began in a scene in the Austrian Alps reminiscent of *The Sound of Music*. We were married in Vernon, BC, Canada, on November 28, 1980. I quickly fell in love with Luba's parents. Her dad owned a 160-acre farm in Armstrong, BC, and we loved visiting her parents once or twice a year. Luba's mom was a wonderful cook and would always feed us no matter what time of night we arrived. Luba's mom also had an incredible memory about her life in Russia and China, and we loved hearing all the tales of her family's trek to Australia. Luba's grandmother, Nadezda, also lived with them, and one day she told us some amazing stories.

Nadezda began telling us of a fifteen-year-old orphan boy who visited her while they lived in China. As we asked further questions about this boy, he turned out to be my dad, Vanya! As if that weren't a big enough coincidence, Nadezda also told us about how her father and several of her siblings were saved in China. They were led to the Lord by Mitrofan Iliyn, my dad's uncle. At this point, Luba and I were sitting on the edge of our seats, hearing of God's involvement in our lives even before we were born.

Then we heard the final story that confirmed God's clear call on our life as a couple. Luba was born on November 26, 1958, in the Singkiang province of China. Shortly after the birth of Luba's younger brother, Alex, her family began the long journey to Shanghai, and eventually to Australia. Luba was two and a half years old as they approached the city of Lanzhou. There was a severe outbreak of cholera throughout China at the time, and apparently Luba contracted the disease. While in Lanzhou, Luba stopped breathing. She started turning blue as her uncle, a doctor, tried reviving her. After fifteen minutes, her uncle informed Luba's parents that their daughter was dead. Luba's dad and mom and all the others in their group began calling out to God. A woman, who is presently still living in Canada, spoke prophetically. "Pray for Luba, don't give up. I will raise her up because she still has great things to do for Me."

Immediately after the prayer Luba began to breathe normally and to this day has shown no lasting effects of her illness. Luba and I walked away that day after hearing this story knowing that God's hand was not only on our marriage but also on our ministry.

We knew early on in our marriage that both of us had a clear call from God to our Slavic people around the world. We have since traveled to more than seventy-five countries, including every Slavic/Russian country in the world. Everywhere we have gone, people have implored us to teach them about marriage and family life. I have told my dad's story throughout our travels, bringing hope and encouragement to every listener. People have begged me to write this story in book form and to make sure it is translated into their language. I do hope this book will be used of God to bring hope to the hurting and encourage people to never give up, to never get bitter at God, no matter what life throws at them.

Sometime after the birth of our four children (Lana Marie, Daniel Josiah, Paul Andrew, and David James), Luba threw a surprise fortieth birthday party for me. She had invited 140 guests, including my dad and mom. Toward the end of the party, my dad, who still couldn't speak English very well, stood and addressed me in Russian. I attempted to translate what he said, trying very hard not to cry, at which I was not very successful!

"Son," he said, "you remind me of Joshua, with a sword in your hands fighting the enemy face-to-face down in the valley. I promise you as long as I am alive, I will be your Moses, standing at the top of the mountain with my hands held high, interceding for you and trusting God for your victory."

Though Dad was never formally educated, he was deeply educated in the ways of God. He still often wakes up early and can't go back to sleep. And so he falls on his knees and begins interceding for his six married children and their spouses, and for his eighteen grandchildren. During frequent family gatherings, my dad always has a speech before we feast on Mom's incredible fare. His speech is always the same, not because he has nothing new to say, but because it is his life message. As the eldest son, I am always called upon to translate Dad's message into English.

> Children, I am so grateful to God for allowing me to meet and marry your mother. I love her so very much. She is my dove, my sweetheart, my greatest joy. I thank God daily for allowing me and your mother to immigrate to this great country of America! I am also grateful to God for giving me six wonderful children and their spouses. And I thank God every day for all of my eighteen grandchildren. Your mother and I pray for you every day. We are trusting God that not only will you and your children be with us for eternity in heaven but also your children's children's children's children will be with us as well.

I'm sure you can detect my father's life message: GRATEFULNESS. Yes, he had a most difficult life, and yes, he saw many miracles. But the greatest gift my father gave us as children was his undying love for God and for our mother and his spirit of gratefulness to God, no matter what he was experiencing.

As his eldest son, I wish to honor my dad for being such a wonderful example to us of a loving father, husband, teacher, pastor, and friend. I speak for all my siblings when I say, "Thanks, Dad! You kept your promise to God, and your story lives on!"

Vanya in Shanghai, May 1947

Vanya and Lena, Shanghai, May 1947

Maria and Lena, Shanghai, May 1947

Shanghai, fall 1948. Clockwise from top left: Vanya, Lena, Maria, and Mitrofan.

Hwa-Lien refugee ship en route to Tubabao, the Philippines, January 1949

Holding coconuts in Tubabao, the Philippines, January 1949. Lena is the first person standing on the left. Vanya is the second person sitting from the left.

Church choir in the Tubabao refugee camp, 1949. Circled in back row: Mitrofan and Vanya. Middle row: Alex Shevchenko, Joseph and Marusia Lokteff. Front row: Lena.

USS *Marine Jumper* en route to Europe, September 23, 1949

Sofia Neciuk, Vanya's future wife, Paraguay, 1947

Anatoly and Lena Kozaczuk, August 13, 1950

Vanya and Sofia, January 14, 1951

Family portrait, January 14, 1951. Standing: Sofia's family, Maria, and Mitrofan.
Sitting: Sofia and Vanya.

Vanya's shoe store in Carmen del Paraná, Paraguay, 1954

Sofia, Vanya, Mitrofan, and Maria with Vera and Peter (author), spring 1955

Marusia and Joseph, shortly before the 1978 car accident that took Marusia's life

Vanya, Misha, and Lena, January 14, 2001. Used by permission.

Vanya celebrating his eightieth birthday with his six children, November 15, 2008.
From left to right: John, Lily, Rita, Paul, Vanya, Vera, and Peter (author).

Vanya and Sofia Iliyn, 2009

PETER ILIYN was born in Paraguay to parents who emigrated from Russia. Raised in the Russian culture and language, he continued his education at the University of California, Berkeley, where he earned his BS in electrical engineering and material science. Peter joined Youth With A Mission (YWAM) in 1976, and has been able to cross barriers throughout the former Soviet Union and Eastern Europe with his ministry. Peter has traveled and ministered in over seventy-five countries across Asia, South America, Australia, and throughout Eastern and Western Europe. Currently he is the North American Director for YWAM. He and his wife Luba have four children and live in Jefferson, Oregon.

For speaking engagements, please contact: pete.luba@gmail.com